Sometimes you've got to

SHOUT TO BE HEARD

Stories from Young People in Care

About getting heard, using Advocates
and making Complaints.

D1331832

Voice for the Child in Care

SHOUT TO BE HEARD – A VCC PUBLICATION

Editor	Tamsin Growney
Voice for the Child in Care Project Team	
Project Co-ordinator	John Kemmis
Assisted by	Judy Templeton
Section on Your Rights	Nicola Wyld
Readers on behalf of 'Shout for Action'	Shafeen Rafiq
	Michael Ryan

Acknowledgements

These stories are written by young people who remain anonymous. All names have been changed. The poems and pictures are also by Looked After young people. VCC wishes to record its thanks to each individual young person who has contributed their story or submitted a poem or picture.

VCC wishes to acknowledge financial support from the Calouste Gulbenkian Foundation which provided the main grant for this project. Thanks also to the Planned Environment Therapy Trust and the Glanmoor Trust for their grants.

VCC also wishes to acknowledge the contribution of the advocates who supported the young people in telling their stories and helped with this project.

Designer	F D Yocum
Photographers	Gina Glover, Photofusion
	John Kemmis

The photographs are of young people who volunteered as models and are not in care

Published by
Voice for the Child in Care
Unit 4, Pride Court
80/82 White Lion Street
London N1 9PF
0171 833 5792

Printed by
Futura Printing Ltd
21 Perseverance Works
38 Kingsland Road
London E2 8DD
0171 739 4995

© Voice for the Child in Care, 1998

ISBN 0 9534407 0 2

contents

Foreword

I am pleased that Voice for the Child in Care has put together this booklet. The stories in it will, I hope, encourage young people to make themselves heard.

Life is not always easy for children being looked after by Local Authorities. Life has had more than the usual ups and downs for the young people who will read this. It is important that all those who work with looked after children should listen to them and take their concerns seriously. That is a message which the Government is working hard to get across. It is a key theme of our "Quality Protects" programme.

Voice for the Child in Care has done some good work in speaking up for the children in the past. The booklet will be of help to you if you have a need for someone to speak up for you. I hope that it will encourage you to feel that you are not alone. We care, and we want the very best for all our young people.

Paul Boateng
Parliamentary Under Secretary of State

Being in care

I don't want to talk **ABOUT IT**.

I don't want to say anything.

Thinking about it **HURTS ME**.

Hicham Aged 10

Introduction

An intimate and painful time in the lives of twenty-one young people is shared with us in this book. All their names have been changed to protect their privacy. My name has not been changed as I share my story with you now.

Having been in care myself I remember the huge feeling of wanting to help others and I feel the young people in this book want to help other children in care.

I am an advocate and am training to be a solicitor. Social Services listened to me twelve years ago when I told them I wanted to stay with my two brothers and we've lived happily with our large foster family ever since.

I remember speaking with the young person called Oliver as we had had such different lives but shared two things in common; our grief for the loss of a parent and that our brothers and sisters meant the world to us.

We have formed a group of young people who have received help from Voice for the Child in Care or have got to know VCC. Some have used the VCC advocacy service and some have used the complaints procedure. We have written this book to show other young people in care that they can get help and get their voices heard. We want to tell those who have power over the lives of children in care how difficult life can be for us and how they could make it better.

> SHAFEEN (aged 24) on behalf of
> Shout for Action - "Those with experience of care
> fighting for those in care."

Choices

I've had my fair share
Wrong or right, I've made
Them all, When everything was
Going well my way I got given a
Choice, but I chose wrong.

But how was I to know, it affected
Me for the rest of my life and
Now there is one way out, make
The right choice.

Tony Aged 15
poem and picture

CONTEXT OF THIS BOOK

The stories are nearly all written by young people who have been in care and used a VCC advocate, or they have been written by the advocate and the young person together.

VCC advocates are professionals who are committed to children getting their voices heard and receive training and support from VCC. Some, like Shafeen, have had experience of being in care themselves.

These stories are written by young people aged twelve and upwards. They describe some harrowing incidents and are aimed at this age group, rather than the younger reader. We have put the short accounts first and the longer ones second. At the end we have drawn together the views of the group, Shout for Action, and put our recommendations forward to the Government to ensure that children and young people's voices get heard and the care system is improved. Finally, we have included information about your rights under the Children Act and listed telephone numbers where you can get help.

The stories are what the authors wished to say. We know that many young people have much better experiences. Many children in the care system are very positive about their carers and their social workers. We hope that all those committed carers and professionals will understand this is not a criticism of you. Nevertheless, many in the work may not appreciate just how difficult it can be for young people Looked After by the state to get heard when things are going wrong.

The most important message of this book is that – even when things are very bad, it is possible to turn things around. When you are young it is not always possible to do this on your own. It is a good idea to talk to a trusted friend and it is OK to pick up the phone and ring organisations listed at the back of this book for help. They can help – you can get heard – things can get better.

Short
Stories

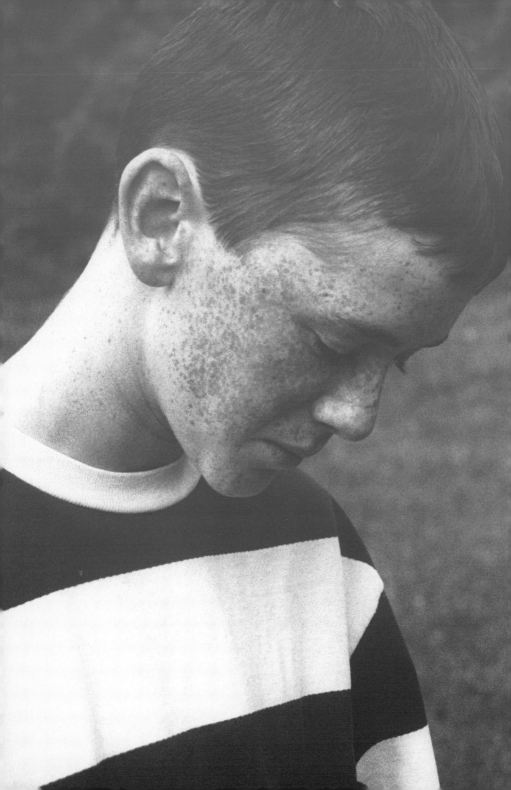

"We're settled now – why can't we stay?"

IAN AND ROBBY

Ian and Robby are brothers. Ian is fourteen and Robby is twelve years old. A year ago there was a plan to move them from their foster home. They wanted to stay, and their foster parents got an **advocate** from VCC to help them.

Advocate
A person who knows about your rights and is totally on your side. It is up to you whether or not you have one.

ABOUT OURSELVES

Ian: "I was ten years old when I came to my foster home. I was very quiet and shy until I came here. I enjoy fishing. I've won some fishing trophies – one big one and two little ones."

Robby: "I'm twelve years old and I'm shorter than Ian. I enjoy football and fishing. I was nine years old when I came to my foster home."

GETTING SETTLED

Our mother died three years ago and our aunt and sister tried to look after us. They couldn't cope and we got put in care.

Care Plan
When you come into care, Social Services must make a written plan about how you will be cared for. They must listen to your views before making the plan. They should give you a copy of your care plan, written in a way you understand.

We were placed in a children's home and then we were moved to our foster home. We felt scared and angry when we were moved. But we settled in and we ex-

9

pected to stay here until we grew up. Our **Care Plan** said that we would stay in our foster home "with a view to permanency". We planted a tree in a local cemetery in memory of our mother.

THE BOMBSHELL

Our social worker told our foster carers about Social Services' plan to move us. He said he didn't agree with the plan but that he was being told he had to move us. He did explain that we had rights.

This bombshell fell and it was a very difficult time.

GETTING HELP

We got a woman called Mary from VCC to help us. She asked us what *we* wanted, and then went to speak to Social Services. Mary came to our **review meetings**. If we didn't understand anything she explained it to us. We usually found these meetings very difficult – just the two of us, with six or seven adults.

Mary helped Social Services and the fostering agency to come to an agreement about money, and we were allowed to stay in our foster home.

OUR ADVICE

We didn't really understand what was going on, but having Mary helped. Our advice to other children in our situation is, believe in yourself and in the people you trust.

Review meetings

At a review, Social Services talk about your Care Plan and how it is working. They might decide to make changes to it. You should normally be invited to take part in the meeting.

"I had already lost one family and home"

LIEAN

Liean was a sixteen year old refugee from Ethiopia. She had lost all contact with her parents in the war in her country, and was brought up by her brother from the age of seven. Her brother decided to send her to England for safety and so he put her on a plane. Liean arrived at Heathrow Airport, completely alone and unable to speak English. She was accepted as a **refugee** and was placed in a private children's home. She settled in the local school, quickly learnt to speak and write English, and started her mock GCSEs.

Refugee

If you have left your country because of danger then you are a refugee. If you come to Britain, the British government decides whether or not you were really in danger before they let you stay

PUTTING DOWN ROOTS

It took Social Services three months to get Liean a social worker and to hold a meeting about how she should be cared for. They decided Liean should go to a foster home. When the foster home plan didn't work out, Social Services told her she would have to move from the private children's home to another children's home, owned by the local authority.

But during her time at the children's home Liean had made friends and put down roots there. The new home was a long way away and would have meant changing school or a very long and difficult journey every day. Liean was injured when she was a small child and the injury made her slow at walking and getting around. All Liean's friends and caring adults were in her children's home and in her school. She was very upset about possibly losing her friends and falling behind with her studies.

"YOU HAVE TO MOVE"

"First I spoke to my social worker, who refused to listen and told me, you have to move or you will be thrown out and no-one will have responsibility for you. She said Social Services wouldn't pay for me if I refused to move and I would be on the street.

"I had already lost my family and home in Ethiopia. The children's home, where I was living, had been my only stable home since arriving in this country. I felt that Social Services did not care about my feelings and my needs because I was a refugee.

FORMAL COMPLAINT

"The next day I was crying in school and my school teacher spoke to me and gave me details of ChildLine, who I rang that evening. ChildLine put me onto VCC.

"VCC immediately provided an advocate and made a formal complaint about what was happening. VCC stopped me being moved while the complaint was looked into. A meeting was arranged with an independent person, my advocate, an interpreter and me. The independent person wrote a report which said that Social Services had handled things badly. It recommended that they think again about my situation."

Liean completed her GCSEs and went to college to study.

THE OUTCOME

It was agreed that Liean could stay at the private children's home at least until after her GCSEs, and then look for more independent accommodation. She was also given a new social worker, who listens to her. Liean completed her GCSEs and went to college to study. She continues to do very well.

Moving Home

My foster home has been great,
Over the years I have improved,
Vases are all over my house,
I love my toys in my house,
Nothing better has happened to me,
Going home is a good thing to do.

Having a home is great,
Once I didn't have a home,
My mum decided to buy a home,
Even though I wasn't there.

Thomas aged 11

"I just wanted to be with Kay and Bert."

AMY

Amy was ten, nearly eleven, when this story took place.
She tells her story with the help of an interviewer.

FEELING SAFE AND CARED ABOUT

Amy was placed with her foster carers Kay and Bert in the summer, and immediately took to her foster home. There was one other foster child, aged fourteen, with whom she got on. She had been having a very difficult time at home before going into care. It was a big relief to be in a family where she felt safe and cared about. She says, "I just loved it here. I loved the dogs; there were six puppies."

Amy carried on at the same school she had been going to when she was living at home, which meant travelling ten miles each day. Kay took her to the school in a taxi. She was a shy girl but she settled down and was doing well at school.

BAD NEWS

Amy remembers the first time she became aware that she might be taken away from Kay and Bert: "I was at the Social Services office one day and then someone there said to me, 'Do you realise you are at a **short-term placement**?'"

Short-term placement In the autumn, Social Services told Kay that
This means that Social Services have found you a home for the time being, but may move you when they find something more permanent.

they'd found another foster home for Amy, nearer her school and her mum. They said they needed to move Amy because she was costing them too much money where she was.

Amy was very worried. She had nightmares. She became pale and ill and her schooling began to suffer.

Amy and Kay talked to Amy's dad about the problem. He contacted VCC, who tried to arrange an advocate for Amy. But the Social Services refused to let Amy see an advocate from the VCC. They said they would find Amy an advocate themselves, but they never did.

"DON'T LET THEM TAKE ME!"

When the social worker came to take her to the new foster home, Amy threw herself on the floor screaming and then ran to the bathroom. She says, "I ran in there so I could lock myself in. It was the only room in the house with a lock. They waited outside the door for a long time, but I wouldn't come out till they'd gone."

The social worker and her assistant took all Amy's clothes and other possessions and left her with nothing - not even her nightdress. After they'd gone Kay and Bert had to buy her a new nightdress and other things she needed.

For a while Amy didn't go back to school in case they picked her up from there. Her social worker then promised not to pick her up from school. So Amy started going to school again.

"They promised me they would not take me from the school," Amy says. "Then, a few days later, the social work assistant met me at the school instead of the person that normally came. She said, 'Come with me, I'm taking you to a new place.' I was so shocked I went with her. I should have run back into the school. I got in the car and started crying.

"We went to the Social Services office. I saw Kay in a room. I tried to open the door but couldn't. I kept banging on the door. Then a lady said, 'Open the door or she'll break it.' I ran to Kay and clung to her."

Amy was screaming, "Don't let them take me!", but the social worker told Kay to let her go. Kay was also distressed and sobbed all the way home.

THE NEW FOSTER HOME

Amy says, "I didn't really understand. Kay left. They were just standing around and then they took me to see my mother. After that, I was taken to my new foster home. They took me upstairs and all my stuff was there in big black plastic bags. The bedroom was small - a box room really - and I was sharing it with a teenage girl. We could only just fit in to it. She was all right. I told her I was not staying, I was going to go back. The house had wood everywhere, even in the toilet. When we had our first meal I said, "I'm not going to eat it," but then I felt hungry and I did eat something.

I didn't want to get to know these new foster carers. They were all right, but I just wanted to go home to Kay and Bert.

Nobody explained to me why all this was happening, but they told me I was to live at this new home. I was told it was too much money for the taxi back and forward from school and Kay and Bert were just too far."

RUNNING AWAY

Kay and Bert were told they couldn't visit or telephone Amy. When they sent their daughter to deliver a birthday present for her, they got told off.

"They sent me back to my school but then when it was coming up to my birthday I wanted to go back to Kay and Bert, so I tried to walk there from school with my friend."

It was ten miles and it took three hours. It was dark by the time they arrived. Kay gave Amy and her friend some tea and phoned Social Services. Social Services told Kay that she had to take Amy to the police station. At the police station Amy was told off for running away.

"After that I was grounded. When I came home from school I

had to go straight upstairs to my bedroom and could only come down for dinner. She only made me do that for two days and on the third she let me come down again.

"I realise it was dangerous walking along the road. I just wanted to show them what I wanted. The social worker did come round often but I wouldn't talk to her."

MAKING A COMPLAINT AND GETTING A RESULT

Kay and Bert and Amy's dad made a formal complaint. The complaint was looked into, and Social Services then applied for a Care Order. Amy was given a **guardian**, who talked to her about what she wanted and why she wasn't allowed to go back to Kay and Bert.

Guardian
Someone chosen by the court whose job it is to recommend who should look after you.

After this Amy's social worker was changed. A Care Order was made and contact with Kay and Bert began again at Easter. Amy went back to live with them in July. She had been away eight months.

She says, "When I was told I was going back I felt glad but I wasn't sure that it was going to happen." When she finally returned she was just so pleased she kissed Kay and Bert and wouldn't let them go. They said she almost strangled them, she was so happy.

Amy is now settled down with Kay and Bert and goes to the local school - no taxis!

"CHILDREN SHOULD HAVE A RIGHT TO HELP"

"When I got moved I felt helpless, no-one listened to me, no-one ever apologised to me. In the end I got what I wanted, but I shouldn't have been taken away. I should have been allowed to talk to an advocate. It could have made a difference. Children should have a right to help if they need it."

"I'm not staying!"

EMMA

Emma is sixteen. She has seven brothers and sisters. She has left school and is studying to be a hair stylist. Emma tells her story with help from her mum.

I MISSED SOME SCHOOL AND GOT PUT INTO CARE

I lived in London until I was fourteen. I was doing OK at home, although I had missed some school. Then Social Services took us all to court and the court put me into care. I said I wouldn't go, and I went home with my mum.

My social worker turned up with the police and I was taken away. They put my youngest brother and little sister in one foster home, my brother Paul, who's a year younger than me, in another, and I was placed in a third home – all in different parts of Kent. I felt really upset. I asked to be put with my brother or the little ones but they wouldn't do this.

RUNNING AWAY

My foster carer seemed really snobby. She told me that my clothes were dirty and that I should have a bath and get changed. I went in the bathroom, ran a bath, then jumped out of the window and nearly landed in their fishpond.

I walked along the motorway and phoned my mum. She was

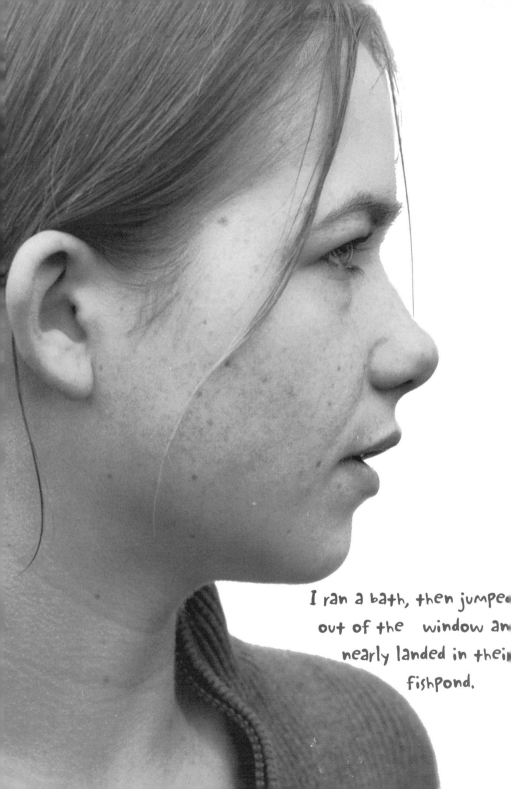

I ran a bath, then jumped
out of the window and
nearly landed in their
fishpond.

scared because of where I was and said that she'd send the police to get me. I didn't hang around; I walked across a hill and found the train station.

They picked me up from home and took me to another foster home. I stayed a day this time. I had some money so I took a cab to the station and went home again. I was picked up and taken back. I ran away from there twice more and then they took me to another foster home.

The foster mother was out at work and the foster father was at home. I found him really weird and didn't like him. I ran away from them and phoned my nan. She said she couldn't help so I ran away again. This time I met my brother Paul and we ran away back home together. The police got us and took us to the police station. I said I wasn't happy going back to the foster home I was at. They said I could go somewhere else. Then, three hours later, the foster father arrived. He locked me in the back of the car, and took me back. As soon as we arrived and got out of the car I ran away.

They took me to another foster home. The carers were nice, and I stayed a day and a half. I talked to the foster mum, but then I said I wasn't staying, I wanted to go home. She said, "I understand : I can't stop you."

HOW I MANAGED TO GET HOME

My nan lived by the seaside and I went down there. I met my mum there and we went into the local Social Services. In the waiting room they had pamphlets and I found one about VCC and got in touch with them. An advocate came to see me and talked to me.

The advocate gave me advice and tried to help get me out of care. She came to the court with me. She stayed with me most of the eight days of the court hearing. She supported me while it was going on, she was really kind and bought me drinks while I was waiting.

The court still made a Care Order on me, and my two brothers and sister. But after the court, the advocate came to see my social worker and persuaded Social Services that I could stay with my mum. So I got the main thing I wanted.

After a while my brother Paul ran away, and then he was allowed to come home too.

GETTING JUSTICE FOR ME AND MY FAMILY

Social Services accepted I could stay with my mum and my advocate said goodbye but then, after I'd been at home for a year, I asked if I could get rid of the Care Order. My social worker said it wasn't down to her, it was up to the court. I saw my solicitor and asked about revoking the Care Order. He applied for legal aid and we are about to go to court.

Revoke
If a care order is revoked it means that it is cancelled.

Also I was really upset because I wasn't hardly able to see my little brother and sister. Me and my mum are allowed supervised contact four times a year.

Legal aid
This means that the government pays for you to have a solicitor.

I've contacted VCC again and asked for an advocate. They explained the complaints procedure. I'm now making a formal complaint about the way we've all been treated. I understand the procedure and I'm going to use it to get justice for me and my family.

Formal complaint
You have the right to have your complaint looked into by an independent person, i.e. someone who doesn't work for Social Services.

I'm pleased I'm back home but I don't think my brother and sister should still be away. I will only be happy when my brother and sister come home. Meanwhile I'd like to be able to visit them much more often.

"Our foster mother did not understand us"

RAUEENA

Raueena is a fifteen year old Asian girl. She and her older sister were both on a **Care Order** and living with white foster carers.

THE WORST YEAR OF OUR LIVES

We had been living in this foster home for a year and were unhappy there. The foster mother did not understand us and we wanted an Asian foster home. We told our social worker but nothing happened. She told us we were only there for a short time, but a whole year passed. We were lonely and upset. It was the worst year of our whole lives. I felt like our social worker wasn't listening to us.

Care Order
A Care Order is when the court decides you should be in care.

GETTING HELP

We found out about VCC and called them from a telephone box. They arranged for an advocate to meet us in the town, away from our foster home.

We talked to the advocate about what we wanted. She came with us to a meeting with our social worker and the so-

The advocate pushed the social worker to get off her backside.

23

licitor who had been involved in the care case. The advocate then asked Social Services to look for what they called an **"out of county placement"**. This was agreed and within a few weeks they found an Asian foster home.

RESULT!

They found us a new foster home. The advocate pushed the social worker to get off her backside and get us an Asian family.

Out of county placement

This is a term used by social workers when you are sent to live somewhere outside your local authority.

Moving Placement

Moving placement is very hard
You don't run your life off a piece of card
Take this one and only chance
And go the full distance
Moving placements is very hard
So don't sit around like a lump of lard
Think ahead and start to grin
Moving placement is a place to begin
Moving placement is very hard
So don't run your life off a piece of card.

Heather Aged 12
picture and poem

Moving Placement

At first I lived with my Mom and Dad
What a bad life I thought I had, then I
Moved to my Grandad's flat, they wouldn't
Leave me alone, not a chance of that.

Three weeks later I'm on the run, every
Body thought I did it for fun, very soon
I was in a children's home, it was silly
I was left to roam, a month gone by
Always running away, no-one knew where I
Was each day.

Then I went to a foster Mom, three
Placements in fact, I was thrown around
Like a bomb, Weoley Castle and Chelmsley
Wood, Harborne, I'd like to stay there I
Wish I could.

I got my money and did a runner, this
Was my last chance, what a bummer.
Now I'm in Secure, it's not nice you see
But the social services couldn't let me be.

Natalie Aged 15

"Not being listened to was driving me mad"

KATE, SARAH AND LUKE

Kate is seventeen and has been in care for the past six years. She used the complaints procedure and the VCC Advocacy Service to challenge plans to send her younger brother back home. Kate includes her sister Sarah's comments in her story.

LIFE AT HOME

My mum and stepdad were alcoholic. He used to beat up my mother and she was suicidal. They neglected Sarah and Luke, my younger brother and sister, as well as me. One day my stepfather smashed up the house and our social worker placed us in a children's home. We only stayed there one night and the next day went to stay with Angela, a foster carer. We arrived one week before my twelfth birthday.

FIRST COMPLAINT

I got on all right until about two years later, when Social Services were planning to move us, and get my younger brother, Luke, adopted. I made a complaint and someone was sent from VCC to be independent and listen to our views. She listened to us like our social worker should have done. After the complaint was investigated they agreed to keep us all together and leave us with Angela.

NEW SOCIAL WORKERS

About a year later a different Social Services office started to deal with our case. These new social workers didn't really know our history, and they supported my stepfather, who wanted Luke home again. They started to arrange one-night stays at home for Luke, and he was very unhappy. My sister Sarah was very upset. She said, "I was scared for him because he would be back in danger, because our parents might go back to drinking and start fighting and that."

TALKING TO A BRICK WALL

There was an inability to explain: it was like talking to a brick wall. The frustration of not being listened to made me feel I was going mad. But I made another complaint and asked for Jill, the advocate from VCC, to help me again.

Jill phoned up and arranged to come round and talk. Luke was under a lot of stress because his father wanted him home and he really wanted to stay with us in our foster home. Jill listened to us; we talked it through and decided

"The advocate was very good at explaining to kids of different ages in ways they could understand."

what was best and the way to go about it. She was very good at explaining to kids of different ages in ways they could understand. She said to Luke he was like the jam in a sandwich. He was able to tell her clearly, "I don't want to go home!".

VICTORY

My last complaint took Social Services a year to investigate. During the process I was worried in case they assessed me and decided I was mad. In the end they decided I was right. Luke was allowed to stay with us and we were able to stay together until I left to live in my flat.

SARAH'S COMMENT

My sister Sarah was very worried and upset about what might happen to our brother. She said, "I kept seeing pictures of them drinking and fighting. If Luke had gone back the people sending him would have been making a mistake. I thought about it every day, and I thought it would never end. Having an advocate helped me get things off my chest. It felt like people started to listen."

Picture by
David Aged 10

"Where can I leave my son while I study?"

KRISHANE

At the time of her complaint Krishane was nearly eighteen years old and had a fifteen month old son. She had been living with her foster carers for three years. She had lived in various foster homes and children's homes previously. She was due to move into an independent flat when she was eighteen.

A COLLEGE PLACE AND A BABY

Krishane had become pregnant just before her sixteenth birthday. Her social worker had been concerned about her going through with the pregnancy and suggested an abortion but Krishane wanted to keep her baby. She had to give up school two months before her exams. She now wanted to go back into education and take her exams. She applied for a place at college for September and asked her social worker to arrange child care for her son. Her social worker said she would only do this when her college place was confirmed.

When Krishane's college place was confirmed in September she informed her social worker, who then said that her son was unlikely to get a place at such short notice. The social worker asked about the college crèche but the college crèche said that Krishane's son was too young.

31

LACK OF HELP

"I went to Social Services to talk to another social worker, but all they said was, if you have a social worker already then we can't give you any information or advice or help – sorry!

"But someone on the front desk gave me a phone number of an advice service. The woman I spoke to at the advice service said I might be entitled to a child placement and suggested I might like to make a formal complaint about the lack of help from Social Services. If so, she had someone I could ring and talk to – an advocate.

RESOLVING THE PROBLEM

"My advocate phoned me and we made an appointment to meet and talk. A few weeks later my advocate, my foster mother, my social worker, my leaving care worker, the team manager, the head of teenage fostering, my son and I had a meeting to resolve the child placement problem.

"The outcome was that they made a number of promises about future support and one of them was to get the nursery placement for my son. So far, the outcome is fine."

"I could not live with my mother"

SONYA

Sonya is fifteen and of African Caribbean descent. She is an only child and has never known her father. Until last year she was living with her mother, who is a Jehovah's Witness and very strict. Sonya's advocate tells her story.

PRISONER AT HOME

Sonya was more or less a prisoner in her home, forbidden to socialise after school or at weekends. When Sonya's mother was going out, she would lock up the TV, video and telephone so Sonya couldn't use them.

Sonya had gone to Social Services many times, asking to be put into care. Sometimes they said no, other times they told her that if she returned home they could find her something. But they never did. Her mother always refused to co-operate with Social Services.

Sonya could not carry on living with her mother, so she left. After a period of seven months staying with friends and her boyfriend's family, she found herself homeless.

REACHING A COMPROMISE

She contacted ChildLine and was told about a Refuge. She was also put in touch with VCC and given an advocate.

A meeting was arranged with Social Services, who still refused to find Sonya a place in a home or with a foster family. Instead a compromise was made: Social Services agreed they would fund Sonya to stay with a family she knew through some friends of hers. Sonya agreed to this. Social Services agreed to speak to her mother about the arrangement. Sonya agreed to meet her mother at the Social Services office for a "reconciliation meeting".

NEW FAMILY

Sonya moved to the new family. She has managed to continue at her school and is studying for nine GCSEs. She hopes that her relationship with her mother will eventually be repaired.

"I was unhappy with my social worker"

JOSIE

Josie is sixteen years old She was in care for two years, in a foster home. Josie's complaint was about her social worker.

LACK OF CONTACT

I was unhappy with the lack of contact with my social worker. I had seen him only three times during my time in care. I phoned up Social Services and told them I wanted to change social worker.

In response to the phone call I received a letter from the senior social worker saying there would be more frequent contact between my social worker and me.

RUDENESS

My social worker then phoned me and was very aggressive on the phone. He ended the call by hanging up abruptly.

I rang him back so that the matter could be settled in a civil way but he did not pick up the phone. I felt he had only rung me because I had complained about him.

The following day, he phoned up my foster parent, asking her to be present at our next meeting, as he did not want to see me alone.

I rang him back to cancel the meeting. It seemed pointless to have a meeting with Social Services that wasn't confidential.

GETTING AN APOLOGY, AND A NEW SOCIAL WORKER

I phoned up Childline to see if they knew anyone who could assist me and they contacted VCC, who appointed an advocate for me.

The process resulted in a change of social worker within a few days, which is what I had wanted.

My advocate visited me and we discussed the problem. She then wrote a letter to the Complaints Officer. The letter was passed on to the Team Manager.

The Team Manager needed five days to decide whether or not he would let me have a different social worker. At the end of the five days he wrote to me saying that my social worker would be changed.

Also, he told me that he had had a meeting with my social worker to discuss my complaint. He said that the lack of contact was unacceptable and apologised for this. He said it was unacceptable that the social worker was rude to me on the phone.

I Feel

I feel lonely, I feel scared
Can someone please just tell me why

I feel unhappy, I feel pressurised
Can someone please just tell me why.

I feel unloved, I feel like no one cares
Can someone please just tell me why.

I feel confused, I feel insecure
Can someone please just tell me why.

I feel I have no say in important things in my life
Can someone please just tell me why.

Ann Aged 16

"I deserve love and closeness"

HANNAH

Hannah was ten when she came to this country as a refugee. She is now at college studying nursery nursing.

I THOUGHT WE WERE GOING ON HOLIDAY...

My parents came from Eritrea and I was born in Addis Ababa in Ethiopia. My father was a businessman and we were well off and lived in a large house. Then, my father was suddenly imprisoned. A little later, when I was ten years old, my mother sent me to the United Kingdom with my brother and sister aged eleven and thirteen. I thought we were just going away for a holiday but we never returned, and two years later my mother died.

STRANGE FOOD

When we came to this country we were brought by a cousin, who dropped us off with a family in South London. He said he was coming back in a few days; he didn't. We were then taken to Social Services and placed in a foster home, which we hated. We didn't like the food she gave us, which was of her culture. We said we wouldn't stay there, and we were moved to a children's home.

BRENDA

Brenda was the head of the children's home. When I was fourteen years old, Brenda left. I knew she fostered some children from the home, so I asked if I could be looked after by her. She said yes, but that I must ask my social worker. I spoke to both the social worker and her team leader; they said they would look into it. They talked about form filling and the process.

WAITING

When I was fifteen my sister moved out and I really wanted to move out too. We had a couple of meetings and they promised me it would take six months, but at the end of that time I was still waiting and – nothing.

By September, I was sixteen years old and just starting college and wanted to be settled. I wrote to the Director of Social Services. I explained that for the past three years I had been asking to be fostered by Brenda. I said, *"I'm very unhappy about this situation and feel that I deserve to be with Brenda who will give me the love and closeness that I need."*

I received no reply to that letter. At the end of November I got in touch with VCC and an advocate came to see me. My brother had used a VCC advocate to sort out his flat when leaving the home. I told her that I hoped she wouldn't let me down.

FINALLY!

The advocate helped me write another letter – this time, to make a formal complaint. I sent this in December; it was acknowledged and the complaints officer referred it to the Area Manager. In January the complaints officer apologised for the delay in responding to the first letter and referred my second letter to the Area Manager. Then we heard nothing, so in February, with the advocate's help, I wrote another letter asking about progress made on having my complaint investigated and the general lack of communication.

On 14th February an Independent Person was appointed to investigate my complaint. I saw her together with my advocate on 28th February and two days later my social worker telephoned me to say I would be moving to Brenda's home in two weeks time. There was no review meeting or placement planning meeting to discuss the move or the arrangements but I was very pleased to go to Brenda after all that time.

APOLOGY FROM SOCIAL SERVICES

After that, the complaint still carried on. My advocate asked the complaints officer what had happened to the independent person's report. It was a long time being submitted and then even longer being considered by the Assistant Director. It was August before I got a response from Social Services. I then received an apology.

I still felt dissatisfied by their response, the inaccuracies, the time they had taken. I said I wanted to go to review panel. I presented my case with my advocate's help and it went very well. They thanked me for the way I had presented my case and I then received an apology from the Director. She considered that the

delays were regrettable and it had given her the opportunity to look at how her Department handled such cases.

BEING A REFUGEE

I felt discriminated against. I still feel that it was partly to do with being a refugee, that it didn't seem to matter to Social Services how long they took or whether they kept me informed.

I think that having an advocate and making a complaint got me what I wanted. The independent person could see that my complaint was justified and Social Services then responded quickly. In that way it really helped.

MY LIFE NOW

Now I feel I'm doing OK. I'm ambitious and want to make something of my life. I've joined the young people's group at VCC and have been helping train VCC advocates about refugee issues! I want to be a professional, working with children. I'm thinking of becoming a social worker but I would want to get to the top so I could change things.

I'm thinking of becoming a social worker but I would want to get to the top so I could change things.

"I was scared to tell the truth"

MINA

Mina is now seventeen years old. She was nine when she first came into care, and ten when she went to the foster home she describes.

FAMILY BREAK-UP

My mother is Muslim and comes from Bangladesh. My father is part Indian. I was born in this country, in a hospital in London in 1980. For nine years I lived with my mum, three older brothers, my older sister and loads of pets. We had a dog, a cat, a goldfish, budgies, a terrapin and a hamster.

When I was nine years old the family broke up. My three brothers went to my Dad's; me and my sister went to a resource centre – much like a children's home.

After a while I went to a short-stay foster mum and she was quite lovely. She had two sons and a daughter, and I was happy there. She was caring and really sweet, but I had to move on to my long-term placement and then it all changed.

ABUSIVE FOSTER FAMILY

At this second placement, the foster mother and her two daughters would call me names. They would call me "thick, stupid, dunce, bitch". The mother also ran my parents down, saying my

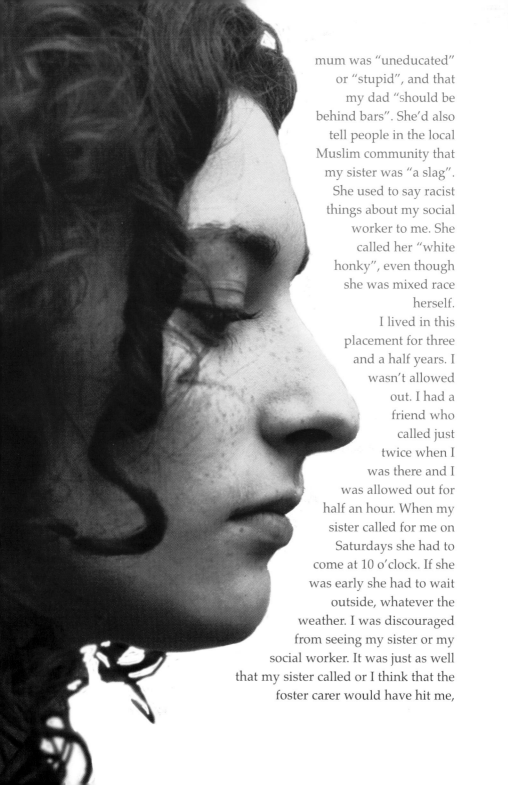

mum was "uneducated" or "stupid", and that my dad "should be behind bars". She'd also tell people in the local Muslim community that my sister was "a slag". She used to say racist things about my social worker to me. She called her "white honky", even though she was mixed race herself.

I lived in this placement for three and a half years. I wasn't allowed out. I had a friend who called just twice when I was there and I was allowed out for half an hour. When my sister called for me on Saturdays she had to come at 10 o'clock. If she was early she had to wait outside, whatever the weather. I was discouraged from seeing my sister or my social worker. It was just as well that my sister called or I think that the foster carer would have hit me, as she did one of the other foster kids.

The family's real daughters were incredibly spiteful towards us foster kids. They would search through my belongings, taking what they wanted and there was nothing I could do about it because the few times I protested the foster mother wouldn't believe me. I had to share a room with the eldest daughter, who didn't want to have an extra bed in her room, so I had to sleep on a chair bed. I was not allowed to spend time alone in the bedroom. As well as going through my things the eldest daughter read my diary. I don't keep one any more.

In the three and a half years that I spent there I didn't go on holiday once. My foster mother told me that Social Services don't give money for my holidays, clothes or pocket money, as she was only paid £5 per week to cover my electricity, food and water, and that I couldn't have any of the treats (foodwise) that were reserved for her real family. She said the money that Social Services gave her didn't stretch to luxuries.

My hair was always long. When I had been there two years, at the age of eleven, the eldest daughter cut it all off. I was really upset and so was my mum.

BEING CALLED A LIAR

I told my social worker about these things, but she then had to bring up the issues with the foster carers. When this happened I would fill with dread and take back everything that I had told my social worker. I know it sounds silly now, because I'm no longer in that situation, but while I was living there, I was petrified of the foster carers. I remember that when my social worker brought up my complaints with the foster carers, the foster mother would turn to me and say, "You're lying again, aren't you? Why do you have to lie about us after all that we try to do to help you not to lie? Why don't you tell her [the social worker] that you're making it up?"

When this happened, I didn't feel that it would get me anywhere if I stood up to the carer and challenged her on what I knew to be *the truth*, because I was too scared of how she and her family would react and what the consequences of speaking out would be. If I complained she would scream and shout at me or get everyone in the household to ignore me. So I would take back my complaints. Therefore the social worker couldn't do anything, as I had given myself a reputation as being a liar.

Even though I wanted to move I was told that there wasn't a suitable placement available for me in borough and if I moved they would probably look out of borough. I didn't want this because I wanted to stay in the same area as my real mother and my sister. So I felt powerless and trapped about everything.

If I complained she would scream and shout at me or get everyone the household to ignore me. So I would take back my complaints.

THE FINAL ROW

Things came to a head one day when the foster mother called me a slag and a slut and screamed really horrible things about my real family. She seemed to have lost control of herself and raised her hand to strike me but hit the cushion on the chair beside me instead. I felt as though my skull would explode at that moment because of what was happening and I felt very scared.

I surprised myself by hearing myself say that I didn't want to live there anymore and that I wanted to move. She surprised me by ringing my social worker. Before my social worker arrived the foster mother said that me and my family were "scum from the gutter". I'd been told things like this many times before, but it hurt that last time because it was said with such poison.

When my social worker came the foster mother was calm, but her daughter started swearing, cursing and screaming really horrible things about me and my social worker. This shocked my social worker and she must have recognised that I had been telling

the truth because I was moved quite quickly into a resource centre until a new foster family could be found.

AN EVEN WORSE PLACEMENT

The new foster family was the worst of all my placements, and I
would go as far as saying that this family were as close to evil as
I've come across. They shredded my self worth down to almost
nothing and they were very good at putting up a united front
when a social worker visited. So it was hard for the social worker
to see what they were really like.

While I was in the placement I saw the foster mother and eldest
daughter beat the two other children in her care. I think that she
would have beat me as well if I had not had contact with my
older sister, who she was wary of. I remember one occasion when
the foster mother punched one of the other foster children (a girl
aged eight or nine) on her mouth, making her bleed, for forgetting to do something menial like emptying the bin or cleaning the
bath. She then screamed at the girl to rinse her mouth and
screamed at her again because she had left blood on the tiles.

The other foster children were younger than me and also terrified
of the family. I asked them to complain with me but they would
just run back and tell the foster carer what I said in the hope that
the family would like them and treat them better (which never
happened). When I left I felt bad that they were left behind.

I told Social Services what went on there and how the family
treated us, but I don't think that anything was done. The foster
mother carried on fostering. I recently came across the local authority's newsletter for foster carers, and saw a picture of some of
the members of this foster family plastered across the front page,
because they have received an award for their service as foster
carers!! I felt a great deal of anger and also sadness when I saw
this, as I know that they didn't deserve to get it.

IF I'D HAD SOMEONE WHO BELIEVED ME...

I know that this sounds unbelievable and I am used to people having a hard time accepting what I've said: only a few people have truly believed me. If you were treated like this in your own family, you would probably have a care order slapped on you, and Social Services buzzing around. But when it's a foster placement, it seems to me to be overlooked. I think that people find it easier to dismiss experiences like mine and label me with emotional problems (a liar), so that they can sleep better at night.

I feel now that maybe, while I was at that placement, if I had had someone outside of Social Services to help me and believe me, then I would have felt confident enough to speak out and not retract my words.

Social Services shouldn't bury their heads in the sand and pretend that everything's fine; children in care need a loving, stable environment to grow strong in, not places where what little dignity you own is robbed off you until you feel like nothing.

"Children in care need a loving, stable environment to grow strong in."

"I knew that I should not be in the secure unit – they'd got it wrong"

ROB

Rob is fourteen years old and an orphan. He has been in care since the age of seven. He has a younger sister, Wendy, who has been adopted by the foster parents with whom she was placed at the age of four. Rob's story is told by his advocate and himself.

THE DEATHS OF ROB AND WENDY'S PARENTS

When Rob was six and Wendy was three, their mother – a heroin addict – died of an overdose.

"I went into the bedroom and saw her lying there. I knew something was wrong but my dad was drunk and when I told him he told me to go back to bed and stop being stupid. So I did. In the morning my dad told Wendy and me that my mum was dead."

Following this, Rob's dad went into rehabilitation for his heroin addiction. Rob and Wendy went into temporary foster care while this was happening.

"My dad came out of rehab and for a while we lived together as a family, until Dad fell asleep and left a chip pan on the stove."

Rob saved his sister and father from the fire caused by the chip pan. When Social Services found out about the fire, Rob and his sister were placed with the foster family again.

"This was too much for my dad. They told us that he had died of a drugs overdose but I know that he killed himself because he was so depressed about losing us after he had tried so hard. Social Services killed him and they're going to pay for it one day."

FOSTER FAMILY

Rob and Wendy then went to live with their foster family long-term and Wendy agreed to let this family adopt her. Rob was angry about this:

"The foster parents are too old and they're going to die and then she'll have to go all through that stuff again. Nobody asked my permission for Wendy to be adopted and I'm her older brother."

Rob stayed on with the family for a while but then he began to run away, and eventually he was removed from the family and lost contact with his sister. He then went from one home to another, each placement breaking down because of his violent temper. He started drinking heavily and sniffing glue.

SECURE ORDER

Following one glue sniffing session, Rob fell off a motorway bridge and was very badly hurt. He spent some time in hospital but eventually recovered and was placed in a secure unit on his release from hospital. Rob had been put in a secure unit before.

When I was younger I use to look after my sister and now I can do that again, she'll let me.

"I knew that I should not be in there this time because they'd got it wrong. My social worker said that I tried to top myself but I didn't. I was just out of it and was having a laugh with my mates. I decided that I would go to court to appeal against the order."

APPEALING AGAINST THE ORDER

Rob found out about VCC's Advocacy Service from the Independent Representative who regularly visited the secure unit in which he had been placed. Rob got in touch with the VCC, and I was appointed his advocate. I found a Children's Panel solicitor and together we went to the secure unit so that Rob could give the solicitor his instructions:

"I told my brief to get me out of there or I'd lose it big time. You couldn't smoke and you weren't allowed to go out or anything."

When the appeal went to court, I requested on behalf of Rob that he be moved to a semi-secure unit in order to assess how he was doing. The local authority agreed to this proposal but, due to staff shortages and holidays, it was delayed a lot.

I was eventually able to negotiate that Rob be returned to the original children's home that he had been in at the time of the glue sniffing incident.

CONTACTING WENDY

I remained in contact with Rob because there was a further issue that he wanted help with.

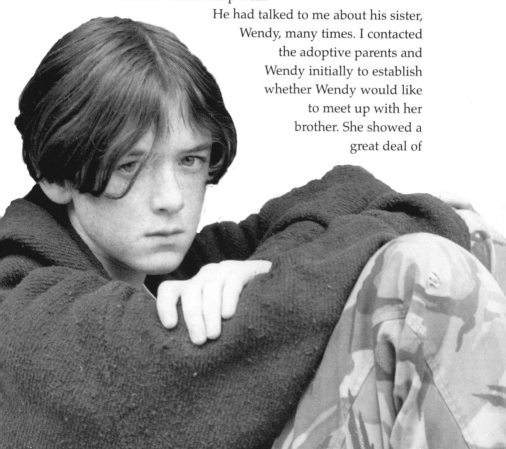

He had talked to me about his sister, Wendy, many times. I contacted the adoptive parents and Wendy initially to establish whether Wendy would like to meet up with her brother. She showed a great deal of interest and it was eventually arranged that I would take Rob down to where his sister lived and that the three of us would go out for the day and see how things went.

"I was very nervous. I didn't know what to expect or whether we'd get on after all this time."

The day was a difficult one, but Rob managed to put his anger towards Wendy's adoptive parents behind him and he and Wendy planned what they would like to do with their day.

One thing they both agreed on was that they wanted to visit their Mum and Dad's gravestones at the crematorium.

At the graveside, all the emotions of the loss they had in common came to a head and they were able to say lots of very honest stuff to each other. Rob explained his fears over the age of Wendy's adoptive parents and she told him not to be so silly.

WHAT'S HAPPENING NOW

Rob continued to show lots of anger towards both peers and members of staff but eventually, as he had wanted all along, a foster home was identified for him and he went to stay there in order to start a new life.

He still maintains long-distance contact with his sister and, although it is happening slowly, they are developing a strong brother-sister relationship.

"When I was younger I used to look out for her and now I can do that again, if she'll let me."

"They take you in as a child, then throw you out at sixteen"

JASMINE

Jasmine came to this country in 1989 from the Middle East. She was put on the Child Protection Register at the age of fourteen.

ME, MY FAMILY AND WHY I WENT INTO CARE

Over the years I had a troubled relationship with my family. There was a lot of fighting and I would often walk out.

One evening, when I was fourteen, I had a fight with my mother and sister. I walked out of the house. My nose was bleeding. A young man came up to me. He seemed concerned about me and was very kind. He invited me back to his house. We spent a long time talking about my situation.

Later on some of his friends arrived. His mood changed and he began to touch me. I was frightened, I was a virgin and had no experience of men. He raped me. After he finished one of his friends also raped me. That night I was raped by four men.

I got home in the early hours of the morning. It was the latest that I had ever been out. My father beat me up. I was too scared to tell anyone what had happened to me. I did not want my parents to find out because for an unmarried girl to lose her virginity in my culture is a bad thing. It means that no one will marry her, and it gives her family a bad name.

I could not forget what had happened. I was ashamed and blamed myself. So I eventually told a teacher that I had been raped. Social Services became involved. I asked them not to tell my parents because of the religious and cultural implications, but they told them anyway. This resulted in even more trouble at home.

LIKE A PRISONER

Not long afterwards, following a breakdown with the family, I was placed with a foster carer for one night. Then I was placed in a local residential unit. The unit was horrible. I felt like a prisoner there. I was there for about three months and they refused to buy me clothes or shoes. I was told that they were not prepared to spend any money on me. They told me that my parents were responsible for giving me money to buy things. I was given £3.26 per week for everything.

The kitchen was kept locked and if a meal was missed the child would have to go without. The unit had a mixed age and sex policy and was also used for young people on bail. I came into contact with people charged with serious offences.

TAKING RISKS

I began to drink and smoke cannabis. I was even given crack on one occasion, which made me violent. When the man who offered it to me began making advances, I attacked him. Using drugs and alcohol was a way of forgetting about everything.

I disliked myself and deliberately placed myself at risk. I would walk in lonely streets at night and get into strange men's cars. I thought that it did not matter what happened to me: I was not a virgin so it did not matter if I was raped. When I was at home my sister would boast about being a virgin and my parents told me that no one would want me for marriage.

Another girl from the unit and I went to an old house with some friends of hers one afternoon. We were smoking and having a laugh. I had taken off my shoes and jacket. I went to the toilet, and when I returned, my shoes and jacket were missing. The others pretended that they did not know where they were. It was freezing cold and snowing. I ended up staying in the house for five days with no food or drink. One of the boys continually harassed me to sleep with him; he even tried to rape me. I only managed to escape because a neighbour heard a noise and the police were called.

THREAT OF HOMELESSNESS

Following this, I was returned home. It was one month before things broke down. I wandered the streets and ended up staying with a friend for four nights. When I left there I had nowhere to go so I went to the police station and was placed in a Bed & Breakfast. I was told to be at the Social Services offices the following morning but not given any money to get there. I had to go begging to get the fare.

When I eventually got to the Social Services Department I was told to return home because there was nowhere available for me to stay. I refused to go home and told them of a local unit that I had heard about through friends. They told me that it was private and that they could not place me there. I refused to leave. They changed their minds and placed me at the local unit, saying that it was only until my social worker returned from leave and a review was set up.

When I was first placed at that unit I had low self esteem and was extremely distressed. Every time that I looked at myself I remembered the rape. I could not bear to see my body so I would not shower or bathe. Staff began to suspect that something was wrong; I was told that I smelled and should shower. To begin with I used to have to force myself to shower; I had to close my eyes.

Gradually things began to improve and I started to like myself and to understand that the things that happened to me in the past were not my fault. The people at the unit helped me to gain confidence in myself and my abilities.

RENEWING CONTACT WITH MY FAMILY

During this time, if I saw my mother in the street she would spit to the side to show me how she felt about me. After not having any contact with my family for over a year, my sister turned up at the unit and invited me to her wedding. I started going back home and seeing my family for a short period, but things broke down again.

About seven months later I bumped into my mother at the doctors. I was five months pregnant and she knew straight away. I had little support from the father and was thinking about a termination. When I told my mother she said that if I went through with the pregnancy I would be cut off.

I eventually had a termination, which was a very bad experience. The drug that I was given to induce the contractions acted very quickly. The pain killers did not work. I got up in the night to go to the toilet and I felt something come out. I was frightened and went back to my bed and the baby came out. I was there with this tiny dead baby.

When I told my mother about my experience she was very sympathetic and supportive. She was there for me. I went back to stay at home because I was getting the support that I needed.

HOPES DASHED

I was happy at home, but I feared that if I stayed there long term things would break down again. I talked to my mother and we decided that I would continue at the unit but that I would visit on weekends. We were hoping that we could rebuild our relationship.

The following day at about 3 pm, as I was getting ready to return to the unit, I got a call from one of the workers at the unit telling me that I *I feel as though Social Services take you in as a child and then throw you when you reach sixteen.*

had to come and collect my things. My placement had been closed. I went straight to the Social Services office, in tears. I warned them that things would break down again if I lived full time with my parents.

Social Services refused to accommodate me because of my age (I was sixteen by then), and they claimed that things were OK at home.

But things got worse again at home. I was constantly arguing and being beaten up, and was self-harming. Over Christmas that year I took an overdose.

BED & BREAKFAST

One evening I came home late and my father beat me up. He told me to leave the following day or he would throw my clothes onto the street. The following day I rang the Social Services Department and told them what had happened and asked for help. I was asked to call back later.

I rang my VCC advocate and explained what had happened. She called the Social Services Department several times, but nothing was offered. It got late and my advocate suggested that I contact the children's refuge. She made a call for me and found out that I fitted the criteria and that they had space for me.

While I was at the **children's refuge**, my advocate carried on trying to have me accommodated, but Social Services refused, saying that I would have to go into a Bed & Breakfast. I had been referred to a housing organisation for young

Children's Refuge

A home where children running away and feeling unsafe can go for up to two weeks.

57

people, and was accepted shortly before the last bust-up with my family, only to be told that Social Services no longer had the funding to pay for it. I tried to meet with the team leader to discuss matters but the meeting was cancelled. A place at a Bed & Breakfast was found for me.

MY EXPERIENCE OF SOCIAL SERVICES

My experience of my local Social Services is that they are not helpful. I feel as though they take you in as a child and then throw you out when you reach sixteen. They talk a lot but do not do anything. They do not look at each person's case separately; they treat everyone the same. All young people are not the same; they are all different and in different situations. They only listen when they do not have to help: when they have to help, they run away and turn against you.

MAKING A COMPLAINT

My advocate helped me to make a complaint about the way that I had been treated over this. It was very important for me to make this complaint as I felt that my Social Services Department were mistreating lots of kids.

My complaint was upheld. I am glad that it was successful. I think that my Social Services Department should treat me and all the other young people better than they do.

Child in Care

Careful you might trip
Help, I'm over here
I thought I was in the world
Look at me Death upon a grave

I have a life to live
Not in the world above

Can I care?
Are you there?
Remember that I'm here.
End the 'secure' life.

Daniel   Aged 12

Drugs Aint Good Love

It started with a puff
Which wasn't enough
So I had a line
Which made me commit a crime
Then I needed to chill so I took a pill.

I bought a bottle of Bud
Which made me feel rough
So I took some crack
To try and get back.

I didn't know what I was doing
On a spiral down to ruin
I woke up in a hospital bed
With voices swimming around my head.

Scared confused surrounded by tubes
Empty inside with nowhere to hide
Two weeks later I ended up inside
With my freedom denied.

SO REMEMBER DRUGS
AINT GOOD LOVE

Roxanne Aged 15

"I've had enough
– listen to me"

RIA

Ria is fifteen years old. She has a twin sister called Megan and a younger sister called Susan. Ria's advocate interviewed Ria, and tells her story.

CHOOSING BETWEEN PARENTS

When Ria's mother left the family home in London to go and live with her new partner, she took Ria and her two sisters with her. But then she asked the girls to choose where they wanted to live. Ria and her younger sister Susan decided they wanted to go back and live with their father in London. Upon hearing this, their mother became very angry and began to hit Susan so hard that Ria had to drag her off. The girls then locked themselves in their bedroom and did not dare come out until the next morning.

Ria and Susan did go to live with their father and his new wife, but this arrangement only lasted for five months. During this period, neither Ria or Susan were allowed to have contact with Ria's twin sister Megan, who was still living with their mother. Still angry with them, their mother moved house and did not let the girls have her new address.

ENDING UP IN A REFUGE

Ria describes the event that led to her leaving her father's house:

"I went on a date and my drink got spiked and I got raped by this boy called Ricki who I kind of knew. I realise now that it was probably the date rape drug that everyone is talking about now, but at that time it wasn't so well known about.

"I got back in the early hours of the morning and my dad and his wife had a go at me, calling me a slag and a slut and a liar when I told them what had happened. On 13th September I ran away and ended up living in the Refuge."

The staff at the Refuge asked Social Services to find Ria somewhere to live because her father refused to let her return home. Ria's father told her that his home was "better off without her". Social Services refused to accommodate Ria and said that she must go back and live with her mother – even though Ria told them that she had been physically abused while living with her mother.

As a result of the situation with her father, Ria began to self-harm and also made two suicide attempts because of the memories of the rape. The Refuge took her to the local hospital, not only because of the self-harming but also because she had developed a serious eating disorder.

ON THE STREETS

After five weeks in hospital, Ria ran away, and began to live on the streets. One day she met a man called Freddie:

"I was sitting by the canal and this man started to talk to me. He asked me if I was homeless, and when I said that I was he said that if I wanted to make some money he could help me. He took me in his car to his place and that is when he injected me with heroin for the first time. He then told me that I would have to pay for the hit by working for him and he sent me down to St Pancras Road in Kings Cross. He stood watching on the other side of the road. The first punter pulled up in his car and I looked over the road to where Freddie was standing. He nodded his head, so I went with the man."

As well as heroin, Freddie also introduced Ria to crack cocaine. "If I wanted crack then I knew where to get it and what I had to do for it. It is just a nice feeling. You are not bothered about anything and you don't care about anything."

Ria became addicted to the drugs, and depended on Freddie, her pimp, to provide them. Ria needed the drugs so much that she would visit Freddie at his home, where he would make her sleep with him.

GOING ROUND IN CIRCLES

Ria wanted to be fostered and helped to come off the drugs, so that she would not be forced to sell sex in order to feed her addiction. But Social Services would not agree to this and kept trying to make her live with her mother.

The same thing started happening again and again: Ria would be picked up by the British Transport Police at Kings Cross Station; they would then contact Social Services, who would send Ria back to her mother's home in a car. Then, almost before the car had left the street where her mother lived, Ria would be out of the house and making her way back to London, either by jumping a train or by partly walking, partly hitching lifts.

Whilst on the streets, Ria kept in touch with her advocate, talking to her from phone boxes.

ASKING FOR HELP

While she was at the Refuge, staff had told Ria about VCC, and she had phoned them and been appointed an advocate. Whilst on the streets, Ria kept in touch with her advocate, talking to her from phone boxes. During one of these conversations Ria asked to meet the advocate, saying that she had had enough, wanted to be placed in foster care and helped with her drug addiction.

The advocate rang a children's home. The staff at the home were worried about letting Ria stay there because if Freddie found out where she was then he might come and see her, and the other young people in the home would be in danger. But they agreed to take Ria for a few days.

The advocate made a formal complaint under the Children Act 1989, on the grounds that Social Services had not listened to Ria and that she was clearly a child in need.

As a result of the complaint the Local Authority took financial responsibility for Ria and her social worker found out about a therapeutic unit, where she could be treated for her drug addiction and eating disorder. Ria went from the children's home to the unit. The unit was out of London so that she was not able to make contact easily with her street life and her pimp.

GETTING BETTER

As Ria began to get better she was allowed to visit her sisters. She got to know her twin sister Megan again. Megan is now allowed to visit her in the unit and stays overnight with her sometimes.

"I was being used as a slave at home"

LISA

Lisa is seventeen and has a baby daughter. She had to get a solicitor to help her put herself into care. She also made a complaint about her social worker and how Social Services hadn't helped her.

LIFE AT HOME

I will begin by telling you about my life at home.

I am the youngest of four children. Life at home was never good. My eldest sister Esme left home as soon as she could. I can remember her being beaten by my mum and dad because she went out with a black boy. My dad thumped her full in the face and she was locked in her bedroom for a couple of days.

My sister Christina was in care at about the age of thirteen because she kept running away or being thrown out by my mother. I saw Christina beaten by my mother on several occasions.

I was made to clean the house from top to bottom everyday from the age of twelve. I was made to do all my own shopping and cooking. I was not allowed to eat any of the food bought for the family. I could only use the cooker if I put money in the meter: I was not given any money for any of this by my mother, although my dad would give me some sometimes. Mum would have a go at me about the food I ate and my appearance – this used to make me physically sick. I lost a lot of weight.

My mother preferred me not to go to school, as this meant I could do the housework and wait on her. On Mondays I definitely couldn't go to school as I had to get her Social money – my name was on the counterfoils. I was never given bus fare for school, which meant a forty-minute walk if I didn't pay for the bus myself. I haven't attended school at all since the middle of the Third Year.

Grandad came to live with us and I had to shop and cook for him, empty his toilet bucket, wash him, help him shave and clean and tidy his room. I love my grandad and wouldn't mind doing these things for him but I still had to do all the other work as well.

DRINK AND DRUGS

My mother and father get drunk often, they are always fighting and the police have been called on many occasions. We would be in our bedrooms, hiding.

I started to drink and take drugs when I was twelve years old. This made life at home easier, because it helped me cope. Now that I am away from home I do not take drugs anymore and only have an occasional drink. I want more for myself than having to drink and take drugs in order for me to cope with living at home and being used as a slave, having to meet everyone else's needs. What about mine?

TRYING TO ESCAPE

Since May 1995 I have run away from home, or been kicked out by my mother, on several occasions. Mum treated me like dirt. One time I ran away and went to stay with my sister Christina. I went to Social Services and spoke to a social worker called Terry. He phoned my mother and she said I could return home, which he told me to do. I stayed with Christina instead. When I had been there for about two and a half months, Christina went to see if she could claim any benefit for me. Shortly after this my mother came to Christina's. I let her in, she hit Christina and started beating me in every room – I couldn't get away from her. She then dragged me home.

Christina telephoned to see if I was all right. She said that she had rung Social Services Emergency, but they said they couldn't do anything unless I contacted them myself. But I couldn't. Christina turned up in a friend's car and I ran out and went back with her.

The next week, Dad came around to Christina's, saying Mum had gone away and asking me to return home, which I did. He then made me clean the house thoroughly, it was really dirty and it stank. Then I had to cook his dinner.

Mum came back, and continued to have goes at me, and at night when she was drunk she would wake me up to have a go at me about the stress I had put her through.

RELATIONSHIP WITH DARREN

After my relationship with Darren started, everything blew up. He was my sister Christina's boyfriend and the father of her child, and then we had a relationship. Christina beat me up while Mum watched. She bruised my face with a shoe and pulled my hair out. The police were called but they said there was nothing they could do.

Things continued like this for a couple of weeks and then I ran away again. I stayed with Tracy, the girlfriend of Jamie, one of Darren's friends. But Jamie then told my mum where I was. The police came at 3.00 am and returned me home. My mum beat me with her fists and then I was locked in my bedroom for four days. I was given a blue bucket to use for a toilet. The windows were nailed closed and the door was locked. The only times I was allowed out were to clean the kitchen under mum's supervision, and for one wash. My mother continued to verbally abuse me all the time – calling me a slag.

PREGNANT, AND SLEEPING ROUGH

I ran off again, with Darren, and we went to a seaside town. On

23rd November 1996 I was picked up by the police and placed in foster care. My mother was told where I was, and phoned during the early hours when I was in bed. I rang her back to say I was OK and didn't want to return home.

The foster carers were lovely but Social Services wouldn't listen to me and said I had to return to London. They never came down to visit or see how I was. By this time I was pregnant. I didn't feel able to be a mother and wanted to have a termination. I made an appointment at the clinic. In the meantime Social Services insisted that my foster mother put me on a train back to London. She took me to the station and left me by the train but I was frightened that when I got to London I would be returned home, so I ran off. I missed my appointment at the clinic and went to stay with Darren.

We slept rough and went to agencies for the homeless. Darren went back to London. I had no money for food. In February I went back to my foster mother, Julia, who'd looked after me be-

fore. She took me in and let me stay there until May, when I turned sixteen. Social Services refused to pay her or me anything. She paid for everything and she bought clothes and things for the baby. I'd like to have stayed there after I was sixteen, but it wasn't right with her getting no money.

CARE ORDER

Julia contacted VCC and a solicitor. A VCC advocate and the solicitor contacted Social Services and insisted on care proceedings so that I would not have to return home. The advocate also helped me lodge a formal complaint about everything that had happened.

The court appointed a Guardian ad Litem called Rose. Rose and the solicitor, Teresa, listened to me. The court got Social Services to give me support. I also got a new social worker, who was supportive. Each month the court made an Interim Care Order, and they finally made a Care Order in August 1997.

ME AND MY DAUGHTER

Although I do receive some help now, I still haven't got the kind of support I need to set up a flat and bring up a baby. I'm living on family credit. I am managing and making a life for my daughter, but it's still tough.

I've now been given a full apology by Social Services, with the manager coming to see me. Social Services pay for the rent at this flat for me and my daughter. My daughter is just wonderful and is the most important person in my life. I plan to go to college and try and catch up on some of the education I've missed and improve my writing skills. I still see my foster carer and at the time of writing this I still have a VCC advocate.

My daughter is just wonderful, the most important person in my life

Now and Then

Then, I was with my friends
Now, I'm with my inmates
Then, I had freedom
Now, I have a yard and a cell
Then, I could smoke
Now, I do my rip
Then, I would rob!
Now, I get robbed!
Then, I would beat people up
Now, I get beaten up
Then, I did drugs
Now, I am doing my cold turkey
Then, I had a name
Now, I have a number

Aaron Aged 16
Poem and picture

"Treated like a number"

HERMIONE

Hermione is seventeen years old and is currently living in a
residential children's unit.

MY CHILDHOOD

My main interests in life have always been smoking weed, music
and aggressive in-line skating. I first got involved with Social
Services at the age of six. This was because my mother considered
it acceptable to beat me and my brother.

I spent most of my childhood in East London. My brother and I
were raised by our mother and did not have any contact with our
father. At a very early age we were left to fend for ourselves while
our mother was at work. During my time at primary school I began to bunk off and hang around with thugs. We would hang
around the local estates and take the piss out of people. We often
got onto buses and caused trouble with conductors and went to
the local market to steal things because we were bored.

MY FIRST JOB

When I was about seven I got to know one dealer. He approached
me and my friends and offered us quite a lot of money just for sitting down and cutting and bagging something that looked like
baby powder. We were shown around the estate, and shown what

we would be cutting and bagging. I started off simply bagging cocaine, but everyone was going to be trained to do more complex things, like cutting and mixing, washing, weighing drugs and cleaning base.

After a year and a half I was offered part money, part base coke payment. I was already smoking weed and 'ash, and because I would be cutting up the coke I would be taking, it didn't seem like a big thing. My first time taking base I thought my nose was going to explode. The pain was a killer, but the rush and the high was mean!! So from then on I took my payment in part money, part weed and base.

There was two aspects in cutting drugs, one was the money and the other was just getting high and forgetting everything that was going on at home. When my mum was hitting me and just jarring my brain, I used to go to work and buy between two and four grams of base coke and just either load up with some friends or just sit on my own getting high.

Taking drugs was easier in secondary school as so many people were already doing drugs, and I knew quite a few people as I used to work with them. I didn't see the point in bunking school, as everything was so easy to get without even leaving the school premises.

NO RULES, NO LIMITS

During secondary school I spent a lot of time moving around the place, from family to residential units. I felt as if I had no rules, no limits, almost as if I was untouchable! I was placed into some good children's homes, but there was also some bad ones. I didn't really get on with my first social worker, but with my second one I felt as if I could be helped. I had met a lot of field and residential social workers who felt that I was nothing more then just a number, the way that they treated me, I just didn't have any respect for them.

From an early age I had a deep resentment against the police. I didn't trust them, and they were always stopping me and my friends. They knew about my involvement with drugs, but they had never been able to arrest me for it. There used to be times when the homes knew that I had weed on me and would call the police, but somehow I managed to get away with it.

BED AND BREAKFAST

I carried on taking weed and base, cutting, washing, bagging for a few more years, just kind of living for the sake of it, until last October. Problems were getting on top of me, I was out of my last home and was back with my family, things were not going well, I felt as if there was no way out for me... so I decide to take an overdose. I was admitted to hospital for four days and was seen by a psychologist. After that I was placed in a Bed & Breakfast for three weeks. I never really stayed there, there wasn't a lot of security and I didn't feel safe.

Most nights I spent riding around the West End and City. I'd ride to Kensington High Street, in the rain, wind and snow, anything to not go back to the B&B. My mum had moved borough, so I was now under a totally new Social Services Department. It was so different from what I was used to that I felt alienated from everyone. My new social worker seemed very cold and uncaring, and I thought that the way that she handled me was very blunt.

I had met a lot of field and residential social workers who felt that I was nothing more then just number, the way that they treated me, I just didn't have any respect for them.

GETTING AN ADVOCATE

On 10th October, after ringing around, I got in touch with VCC, and was given an advocate.

Before my first meeting with my advocate, I was really conscious of what she would think of me, and whether or not she would like me and be able to work with me. My first thoughts of an advocate was that they were very similar to social workers, devil's spawn air heads. Once I met her I relaxed straight away. She seemed to be really at ease with young people, she also had some of the street slang down as well, which gave her some cool points. Someone acceptable to be seen out on the street with!!

My advocate explained her role and what issues she would be taking up in my case. She was there for all my important meetings. When she saw that Social Services weren't looking after my needs, she made them TOTALLY aware of their faults. When it was announced to me that I would be moved, a week before Christmas, to a strange unit, it was my advocate who forced Social Services to stop the move.

picture by
Daniel Aged 17

For Patrick and Mary

OLIVER

Oliver was separated from his younger brother and sister whilst in care. He contacted VCC in 1996, and this led to him writing a letter of complaint to his Social Services Department. In October 1997, still dissatisfied with the response to his letter, he lodged a formal complaint. His advocate tells his story.

A SMALL PART OF THE TRUTH

I was appointed as Oliver's advocate on 31st October 1996, when he was sixteen. My remit was to make representation on his behalf to his Social Services Department. I was trying to ensure that his wishes were clearly expressed, listened to, understood and fully taken into account when decisions were taken.

Oliver would tire of me repeatedly checking what he wanted written or said on his behalf. He would usually nod his head in agreement at my suggestions, then wryly comment on how the sentences I constructed never adequately expressed the true situation. I wish he was here now so he could write his story in his own words. However, I believe he would approve of what I have written, while recognising that it is only a small part of the truth.

TIME WITHOUT STRANGERS

This is written for Patrick and Mary, Oliver's younger brother and sister, who were everything to him. He ached with the longing to be with them, to enjoy them, to have time with them; the special, open-ended time which siblings spend with each other in their childhood, immersed in fairy tales and imaginative play. Oliver remembered this kind of time from his own early childhood, when, in myths, stories, open space, woods and picnics, the seeds of his individuality were sown. Bound up in Oliver's need to spend time with his siblings was his need to find himself again. The time he was asking for was time without strangers, time without an ending, time to find a new beginning for himself.

LIFE IN CARE

Oliver told me that his life had been suddenly turned upside down by allegations that his father had sexually abused his sister. Everything then went from bad to worse. His father took his own life. Oliver became extremely distressed and was admitted to hospital. A few months later he was led to believe he would be going home to his family, but in fact Social Services had applied for a Care Order, and he was placed in care.

His memory of his time in a local children's home was of being constantly watched and not allowed to spend time alone with his family when they visited him. When he was moved from this home he was told that he was going to a really good boarding school and he would be able to go home for holidays. Instead he found himself in a home with children who were very disturbed, attending a local day school, and *not* allowed home for the holidays. He eventually ran away.

Oliver felt that Social Services tried to make out that his mother was not good enough as a mother, but he was very close to her and thought the world of her. Despite her drink problem she gave her children a great deal of attention. His greatest fear was losing her, and his greatest fear came true. She died of pneumonia.

"BAD INFLUENCE"

All three children were taken to a children's home. Soon after, the home closed and Oliver was separated from Patrick and Mary, although placed initially nearby. Mary's new home did not allow smoking, but they gave her no help to deal with withdrawing from nicotine. One day she came to Oliver in tears, and he gave her some cigarettes. From then on he was viewed as a bad influence on her. Soon after, both his brother and sister were moved to separate foster homes some distance away from him. Visiting was

supervised. He didn't feel comfortable during the visits and some months had slipped by without contact.

At the time that he contacted VCC, Oliver was desperate to renew proper contact with his brother and sister. Oliver told me how they had been very close as young children. When they were in a children's home together they liked to spend time just with each other, in order to be a family. Oliver felt that their need for this was not understood by Social Services. When they were separated Oliver asked for more contact but he was told that his brother and sister needed time to settle.

THE IMPORTANCE OF FAMILY

Oliver wrote a letter to his Social Services Department, complaining about the decision to separate him from his siblings and asking to be allowed to see Patrick and Mary unsupervised and more frequently, and for all three of them to be able to meet up together at times.

Once the complaint was made Social Services promised to look into the issue of contact immediately and said they expected it to be sorted out by the end of the year. Oliver did begin to see Patrick from time to time when he was visiting other relatives in London. Despite meetings and discussions and further promises throughout 1997, no other arrangements for contact were actually made. Oliver was not having any contact with Mary, and was told that she was satisfied with the current arrangements. Contact for all three of them together was agreed but never arranged. At no time did Social Services acknowledge the importance for Oliver of being with his family; instead they said that he posed a danger to them. Oliver sometimes said that they had undermined him to the point where *he* did not think he should see his siblings.

Finally he made a visit to his sister, which turned out to be his last. Oliver often smoked cannabis and drank heavily. In February 1998, when he was very drunk, Oliver walked onto a railway track. He was hit by a train and killed instantly. He was seventeen.

"I then became an unruly child"

ALANA
Alana is currently at college studying Humanities and Social Science. She has a seven-year-old son. Last year Alana came into contact with VCC, and began to write the story of her experiences in care. The following is an extract from the story, which formed the basis of her complaint to Social Services.

LIFE AT HOME

From as early as eight years old I begin to notice that mum had a dislike towards me, as she would always beat me. I would go to school with bruises, black eyes, swollen lips. She would find any reason whatsoever to beat me up, i.e. if the washing up wasn't done, if the house was untidy, if her friends said I was growing to become a pretty young lady or that I was prettier than my mum, if I was in the house alone with her boyfriend. She even ask me what was going on between me and her boyfriend if I walked from one room in the house to another in my night-dress; if I spoke about my dad or if I was happy for whatever reason she would beat me.

When this was going on we were in and out of foster care, starting new schools and then leaving again. I then became an unruly child; I began to steal from anybody and everybody, shops, teachers, friends, I would even steal my mum's fags and smoke them in the toilet. We had our own family social worker and I remember on many occasion I would say to him that I didn't want to live with my mum and explain my reasons. He would say that I'm too young to make up my mind what I want and that it would have to be up to my mum to make this decision. I then began to run away from home to my dad's or to my uncle's. I would be allowed to stay there with them for a while then they would send me back just in case the police had been called. When this happened I would get beaten more and more and would be told by her that they didn't want me because if they did they wouldn't have brought me back home. I then began running to Social Services for help but again they would take me back home. I would tell the school who would then inform Social Services, but still be returned home.

All this would result in me getting a good beating, so I stopped talking to anyone about the goings on in my house.

All this would result in me getting a good beating, so I stopped talking to anyone about the goings on in my house.

MRS TURNER'S

I was placed in foster care at Mrs Turner's. I remained with Mrs Turner and her boyfriend Clive for about a year. In that time I was able to come out of the shell I had built around myself and tell Mrs Turner about all the things that my mum would say and do to me. I helped out a lot, i.e. going to the shops, looking after the children that came to stay, cleaning, going to the bank to pick up her money, you name it I did it and I didn't mind at all, until I noticed I was doing everything and not just for her, but for her children and for her boyfriend. I was now becoming fed up and didn't feel I was able to say no, so I put up with it.

BABY ASHTON

As a foster parent Mrs Turner would have many different children from all ages and backgrounds. She would tell the social workers that she had two rooms available when she only had one, the room she was advertising was in fact her son's room. Ashton came when he was just a few weeks old and from about the first week that he moved in he was my responsibility especially when I wasn't at school. I had to make his feeds, change his nappies, take him on walks, which included the betting shop, bath him, put him to bed, take him to the clinic with a note from Mrs Turner lying as to the reason why she wasn't there. When he cried it didn't matter what I was doing; I would get called to come and get him. Mrs Turner loved to sleep in the mornings until about 10 or 11 o'clock, very rarely would she get up early. Ashton would wake up during the night crying for a feed and to be changed. I could hear him from my bedroom, crying his lungs out, and Mrs Turner would not get up and feed him. I would then get Ashton and take him to my room, change him, give him his feed and then put him to sleep with me. I would bring him back to Mrs Turner when I was going to school in the morning, depending on where I was sleeping. (As sometime I would have to sleep down in the living room with him if John came to stay from the Midlands.)

This went on until the day Ashton left. I had done everything for Ashton and I wasn't even allowed to say goodbye (even now I wish I could see him again).

JOHN'S COMPLIMENTS

John as I said before would come at the weekends and on a few occasions for a week or two. John would always pay me compliments about the way I look, the way I would dress, he would always stare when I walked into the room, so I would leave the room. John asked me if I was avoiding him, and as soon as I would say "No", he would start with his compliments. He would say, "If only I was a few years younger..." Then he would ask me if I would have gone out with him. When I said, "No", he would then ask me "Why?". This would really upset me, so all I would say was, " I didn't want to", and walk away. But he would be on my case all the time asking me the same stupid question. Mrs Turner would also have her other friends from the Midlands come to stay at the weekends. They would sleep in my room, so if John was there that weekend I would have to sleep in the living room with him. He would sleep on the two single chairs and I would sleep on the three seater. I would hate this because he would always close the door, or if Mrs Turner came down she would close the door. Those nights I found it hard to sleep, I would lay awake listening to his every movement. In the morning I would wait until everyone was downstairs, and go to my room and sleep if I could.

Mrs Turner would sometimes tell John, "Leave the girl alone you just told her that a few minutes ago." John would then say laughing, "I can't help it she's beautiful, I wish I was a few years younger". Anyway Mrs Turner decided to have a party to which a lot of people were invited including myself. When I came downstairs for the party I went to the front room to see how many people were in there. John was in there so I left. I then went into the kitchen where I stood in between the kitchen sink and the dryer. I was only in the kitchen a few seconds when John came in and started making his compliments towards me. Then he started to move slowly closer towards me saying, "I would love to kiss you", and then he tried to kiss me. I then pushed him away saying "Excuse me", but he wouldn't move, so I said it louder and pushed him at the same time and then he moved. I then ran upstairs crying and didn't bother going to the party.

The next morning I went in to Mrs Turner's bedroom when I heard that her boyfriend Clive had gone downstairs, and told her what John had done. She then said she would have a word with him, so I went back to my room. The next thing I heard was a lot of shouting. John was saying he was sorry, Mrs Turner was saying that she could get in to a lot of trouble if I told my social worker. John again said he was sorry and it would never happen again, also that he would go home that day, but was told by Mrs Turner and Clive that he could stay, which he did. I spent that day in my bedroom and was told by Mrs Turner that John was sorry and he said he wouldn't do it again. She then added that if I told my social worker about this she would lose her job, so I kept it quiet.

FIGHT WITH CLIVE

John was still coming at the weekend so I would spend all my time in my room One evening I went to have a shower and heard a knock on the door, so I turned off the shower to ask who it was. It was Clive asking me to hurry up in the shower as he wanted to have a bath, which I agreed. A few minutes later he was back, but this time he was banging and shouting for me to get out now, so I said to him that when I have finished I would come out and also that he has a bath and shower in his room, so why is he knocking on this door. He then said I was using up all the hot water. The banging stopped, then I heard someone was fiddling with the lock, so I said, "I haven't finished". I jumped out of the shower and put my dressing grown on just a second before he got the door open. Clive then stood at the door with a knife in his hand still telling me to get out. I then said I hadn't finished and started to brush my teeth, and the next thing I knew Clive grabbed my arm and pulled me out of the bathroom. I then started shouting at him to let me go, but he wouldn't so I continued shouting and screaming at me and the toothpaste from my mouth was going on his face. The next thing I knew Clive slapped me around my face and I ran screaming downstairs to Mrs Turner.

I told her every thing that had happened, and she went upstairs to talk to him. I explained everything which included how the toothpaste ended up on his face (that it was not a direct spit in his face as Clive had told Mrs Turner and John).

That night I slept in the front room and John had my room. I'm not sure which children were in there and why. The next morning no one spoke to me. Melissa and Pauline said I was a liar and out of order for spitting in Clive's face and if it was them they would have hit me too. This went on all weekend. I wanted to run away, but couldn't as I had no money.

BREAKDOWN AT MRS TURNER'S

Monday morning I went to my year's common room where my Head of Year was sitting and he asked me what had happened. I remember breaking down in tears and he told everyone to leave the room. I then told him everything. He asked me if I had told my social worker about what had been happening. He phoned her and arranged an appointment.

After school I didn't want to return to Mrs Turner's, so I went to my father's workplace and told him. It upset him and he left work to go down to Mrs Turner's to find out why this had happened. When we got to the house we all sat down and both Mrs Turner and Clive said I was lying, that I always make up stories. When I tried to speak I was told by them to keep quiet. When they had finished my father had believed everything they had said and got up and left. They then came to me and asked me why I had told my dad, then said I was a trouble maker and my own father didn't believe me.

From this day I became a different person. I bunked off school, ran away, came home late, so they took my keys away from me, and if I got home late they wouldn't open the door so I would have to go back where I had came from, or I would ring the doorbell for a long time and shout to them. If they didn't open the door I would call the police. Mrs Turner would then start hiding the food. Mrs Turner always said she wanted a new kitchen, so she got one and had a lock put on the kitchen door and would have it locked all day even if she was in the house and walk around with the key, so I stopped going back there at night and only came back when I needed a change of clothes. I was called ungrateful and told that now they all understand why my mum didn't want me.

After a few weeks a meeting was held and I was then told that as soon as a foster parent comes up I could move. Then a foster parent was found. I went to meet them and moved out of Mrs Turner's a few days later. I couldn't even bring myself to stay there on the last night, and returned there an hour before I was due to leave.

Out of the frying pan

CHRISTINE

Christine was eleven when she went into care. Now she is grown up and has two young children aged three and six months.

ABOUT MYSELF

I come from a large family: there's nine of us including my parents. We were quite a close family, we stood by each other as brothers and sisters. We had a lot of pets. I was a tomboy, I loved getting grubby, playing football, climbing trees, and I liked to wear my baggy jeans and baseball cap.

ALL ON MY OWN

When I was nine I was taken into care because my father had sexually abused my older sisters and physically abused us younger ones.

I was placed in a foster home. I was only there a week and was regretting it already. I asked my mum if I could go back home. The social worker said I was in care until I was eighteen; they had a Care Order.

I was on my own, all my bothers and sisters were in other places. I was scared, so I found myself a favourite corner, where I always sat.

The foster parents treated us foster children differently to their own. I was constantly blamed for things I hadn't done. The foster mother's children would be bought new clothes, but we weren't; we never had anything. She'd go out and buy her kids things and I'd say, "Can I have some new clothes?" She'd say "No". Often I'd ask for my pocket money but she'd say, "No – I've had to buy you clothes". I didn't feel happy and wanted to go home. So I started bunking off school and running away.

ONE BIG, HAPPY, SHORT-STAY FAMILY

I was there about six months, and then my social worker moved me miles away to the coast so I couldn't keep running home. This was a huge foster family. With the foster parents' kids there were fifteen people in the house. There were five or six little children in one bedroom. I had my own room. They were really nice foster parents. It was just one big happy family. We were all treated the same: us, the foster children, as well as their own kids.

I was moved though. I was told it was just short-stay, but I didn't really understand why I was moved. I was taken to another family at another seaside town.

YOU WEREN'T ALLOWED TO SIT ON THE CHAIRS

I hated the place. The foster mum treated her three daughters completely differently to the foster kids. We were told to get up at six. If we were late we got dragged to our seat at table. You were told to keep your hands off the table. You had to talk correctly. If you did something wrong she'd poke you, pull you about, drag you by the hair. She only hit me once. You weren't allowed to sit on the chairs and we were told not to play with her kids' toys. We weren't allowed in the house; we had to be outside or in the conservatory. We were only allowed three drinks a day.

THE FOSTER MUM SAID, "I HATE YOU"

I complained to my social worker. She said she'd talk to the foster mother later. The moment the social worker stepped out of the door the foster mother gave it to us foster kids. She said "I hate you". She just made our lives a misery. She wouldn't let us watch television. Mind you, she didn't let her own children watch much anyway.

We told our parents, and the social worker was sitting there listening, but she never really took any notice. We couldn't really do anything about it. We were never on our own. We weren't allowed to go to the post-box. If we talked at night we were in trouble.

TROUBLE AT SCHOOL

I went to school but I didn't get on. I was a Londoner, a Cockney, and I didn't fit in. I found the schoolwork hard. I kept being put in new schools half way through the term. I did get in quite some trouble at school and I didn't get any help. One of the foster mother's kids said she'd show me what to do. She then told her mother that I'd copied her work and I got into trouble.

A NEW HOME

That foster mother eventually became ill and, aged twelve, I was moved to a foster home with my older brother. At first it wasn't so bad. The foster father kept to himself and took little interest. The foster mother was strict but nice. But after a while I found if you didn't keep on the foster mother's side, she'd be right nasty. She'd make you stand up straight and if you didn't tell the truth she'd wash out your mouth with washing-up liquid. She'd often drag you up to the wall and give you a smack. I was there about a month before I saw her do this to my brother. In some ways I was shocked, but it was what I was used to.

KISSING ME HELLO AS WELL AS GOODBYE

After six months of being there the foster father would take an interest if we were in trouble. My brother was always beating me up and the foster father's own son was sticking up for me. So my brother said he'd get him back. My brother said that their son had been touching me. It was lies. Then a couple of days after that the foster father suddenly kissed me goodbye. I was quite surprised. Then he started kissing me hello as well as goodbye. It went on from there – he came in my room. Then he started sexually abusing me. It just went on.

I didn't feel I could go to my social worker. She'd never believed me in the past. The foster mother knew, but never did anything. I told my brother. After a while he told the foster mother. She beat me up, screaming, "You liar!" and rang my social worker to come and take me away. She threatened to kill me if I repeated the story or said it was true. She poured hot tea over me, hit me with her ashtray and dragged me round the room.

> **I'd been put in care to be protected from my dad, and then I'd suffered worse.**

"WHY DIDN'T YOU TELL US BEFORE?"

When the social worker came down I didn't dare say what had been happening. Instead I said I'd made it up. The social workers told me off for lying about things like that. They told me off for breaking up my foster placements.

When I was in the social workers' car and they were still telling me off, I just burst into tears. I was so relieved to leave that home. I told them that it was true, what they were doing to me. They said, "Why didn't you tell us before?"

I had a police interview and they decided not to prosecute the foster father who had abused me. My social worker thought it would be too traumatic for me.

I never received any help to cope with what had happened to me.

LIVING IN CHILDREN'S HOMES

At the age of fourteen, I was taken to a children's home because I didn't want another foster home.

This children's home was something else. The staff were continually being beaten up, the home was wrecked and the kids were mugging the old people next door. I was bullied. You couldn't have a bath because they'd unlock the door from the outside. There was a time I was bashed by the police. They picked up the lot of us when there was trouble, and they didn't know who was responsible. I was hit on the knuckles with a truncheon when I went for my pocket. They probably thought I had a weapon. There were knives and things in that home. I was strip searched. The staff told the police that I wasn't involved, but I never got any apology. It never occurred to me to make a complaint.

I was then taken to a more secure home. It wasn't a proper secure unit but the doors were bolted at night. I was watched all the time and I wasn't allowed out. I had home tuition. When I did go to school I was taken there and picked up at the end of the day. You weren't allowed to go to the toilet without someone standing outside. All our phone calls were monitored. Letters would be read. You were never allowed any privacy.

FOSTER MUM WHO COULDN'T COPE

Fortunately I then got a new social worker. She was nice and she moved me to a really nice couple with a beautiful house. At last, I thought I was going to be happy. I was able to tell the foster mother about my upsets. But then she started taking new kids, who were terrible. They took drugs, smashed the place up, and she just couldn't cope. She'd wake me up at 11 or 12 o'clock at night to get me up to have a drink with her. She liked her drink and would give me Baileys.

RETURNING HOME

It broke down and I was returned home. I was told that a social worker would come and visit but he only did once. I was fifteen then. The Care Order was discharged two weeks before my sixteenth birthday but I was told I'd still receive support from Social Services.

My return home didn't work out so I was staying with my sister, where I had to sleep on the floor. Then I fell pregnant. I went to my other sisters and various friends. My boyfriend became violent. I asked Social Services to help me. I was hoping for a foster home where I would get help with the baby. Social Services didn't come up with anything so I went down to the Homeless Families Unit. They put me in a Bed & Breakfast. Then Homeless Families put me in a flat before the baby was born. I received no help from my social worker.

I'D BEEN PUT IN CARE TO BE PROTECTED, AND THEN I'D SUFFERED WORSE.

I wanted to make a complaint about what had happened to me in care so I contacted a social worker I had liked and she suggested I ring VCC. I'd never heard of it before. I rang them but I felt nervous because I still felt like a child in care and that nobody would believe me. Still, I knew it had happened and I wanted to do something about it.

I rang them up and then an advocate came round to see me. She was nice, it was so easy to talk to her. I now see my advocate as a friend.

I wanted to know what had happened to the foster father who had abused me. I wanted him behind bars. I wanted to complain about the way my social worker never listened to me and how my life was ruined. I'd been put in care to be protected from my dad, and then I'd suffered worse.

I was awarded criminal compensation for the abuse I had suffered.

The advocate helped me talk to the police about the possibility of a prosecution. She helped me go through the complaints procedure. It took eighteen months before they finally began the formal investigation of my complaints. I often felt like giving up and moving on. But I'm glad I kept going and this was only possible with the help of my advocate.

THE OUTCOME OF MY COMPLAINT

I was awarded criminal compensation for the abuse I had suffered. The **Crown Prosecution Service** refused to prosecute the foster carer who had sexually abused me, but I did discover that he and his wife had stopped fostering. My complaints against Social Services were eventually investigated and I am awaiting the outcome.

Crown Prosecution Service
The Government department which, with the police, decides whether to start a criminal court case.

MY ADVICE

If anything happened to you in care, I'd say, get out and get help. I know I say this now but at the time when you are scared you just can't do it. I didn't know about how to get independent help. They should have independent people who visit the homes and talk to the children on their own to ensure they are all right.

If anything happened to you in care, I'd say, get out and get help.

"Abuse was normal"

MAURICE
Maurice and his brothers were put into care after their mother's death. Maurice is now thirty-seven and runs his own company. He has two children and a third on the way.

CHILD HEAVEN

I was four years of age with one elder brother and two younger brothers. A traumatic childhood due to father's drinking and mother having spent time in homes for battered women. Eventually, isolated in a dingy flat in East End of London, my mother commits suicide – dead.

Suddenly I found myself in a big Victorian institution in the middle of the countryside, a fabulous place, a child heaven, with a swimming pool and gymnasium.

At the child heaven, they made us wear winkle-pickers and black macs to school. After tea, we used to say the rosary. And then, every night, the house mother, with her varicose veins and her drinking, on the pretence of putting us on the potty, taking us out and fondling us

I was bewildered, and completely numb. We weren't told what had happened to our mother or father. We never saw our father for years and years. What is also bizarre is that none of our family (aunts, uncles, grandmother) were ever told where we were.

BEING SMOTHERED

I do believe that our biggest problems stem from the house mother's abuse of us. We developed an unhealthy interest in sexual things at a very early age. We would play doctors and nurses like any other child, but we would be having sex effectively.

My need for affection at that young age was satisfied in a sexual way, and that's all I knew. The only way I knew of getting affection was sexually. Instead of giving love, the staff in the home gave abuse, so as time went by I wanted the abuse; because it was either abuse or nothing. We never got any nurturing or encouragement.

The thing I want to emphasise is the loneliness and the desperation that I felt as a child in this institution. We did not complain. It was so normal for there to be abuse going on that we did not even consider complaining. Who to? The main man on the staff was a perpetrator himself.

I remember that I was quite playful, energetic, lively, and then the light went out. It was like being smothered. I awoke at the age of fifteen with an utter disgust for my being, for everything I was and everything I might be. The only thing there was for me was wanting to die.

INSTEAD OF DYING

Instead of dying I went to the local Christian Club. I had no time for the belief system, especially because of my house mother, the rosary and the abuse. What I did find was some comfort in the generosity of the people there. They were willing to listen to me and to respect me in a way that I wasn't used to.

The other thing I managed to do was befriend an old lady who I used to deliver papers to – to go there for tea and biscuits. She's dead now, but she was wonderful. Someone I really cared about, and who really cared about me.

Because of my relationship with the old lady, and the people at the Christian Club, I was willing to look at myself, and to endeavour to change. I started going to therapy. Coming from an abusive background, you've got the task of redefining who you really are. Otherwise, you are still a prisoner of who you are taught to be. In my heart of hearts my greatest wish was that I would never do what was done to me.

The most important message that I have to give is that there is the possibility that you can again taste happiness. Somewhere inside your being there is that loving, gentle person, and all the bitterness and anger are just sitting on top of it. Once you get down into it, and you've screamed and cried, hit the wall, begun to deal with what sits on top of who you are, then you've got the chance. It is hard work, but it's less painful than allowing yourself to be totally destroyed by what you've experienced. That's the message.

HOPE AND TRUST

You need to come across a person in the world in whom you can find some solace, someone who actually listens to you, whoever it may be, a teacher at school, a friend, whatever. For me I went up to the Christian Club, because I thought I could find someone who cared, but even there I was incredibly suspicious. I just didn't trust anyone, and was always trying to read between the lines. Anybody being nice to me I read as wanting to abuse me.

The hardest thing in the world is to hope and to trust; to overcome the feeling that everyone and everything is just an utter pointless waste. If you can link in with someone and begin to talk about your experiences, then you can gain the strength to move on from them.

The people I know who have isolated themselves are very unhappy, because all they've got is their compulsion. That may be gambling or drinking or sexual things, but that's what they feed on, they feed on what they were taught to feed on. When young people become abusive themselves, they are fulfilling their abusers' prophesy that they are worthless: "I'm not worth anything therefore I'm going to get pissed", or, "I'm not worth anything and I'm going to be a slag".

95

Get out there into the world, link up with what is positive and what is good. Go to the sports club, go to the night clubs. Even if you fail every exam, even if it all amounts to not very much on paper, the mere process of having gone out there and involved yourself in what is the real world changes things.

COMPLAINING

Once I had gained a bit of strength, a bit of self belief, I decided, "Right, I'm going to do something about what happened". Five years ago I made my first complaint. Subsequently I phoned up VCC and was allocated an advocate.

It's been a long and arduous battle; five years is a long time. But I'm expecting to get a result soon. My driving force is the plight of those that have gone before me and those that came with me, all those who are suffering and have suffered due to their experiences in care.

If you know that your complaint is right and true, you have to pursue it. The complaints procedure is still very primitive in most boroughs, but we as young people who have come through the system have a responsibility to all the children who are still in the system, and must pursue our complaints with diligence.

If you know that your complaint is right and true, you have to pursue it.

Getting justice

ANGUS
"I'm Angus. I am now 22 years old. Six years ago I was placed in a residential school by the Social Services for being "out of parental control".

MY NEW "HOME"
My first impression of my new "home" was of a domineering building in sprawling grounds, well facilitated, with a swimming pool, a weight training room and a large gymnasium. I was placed in the "open" unit, where I had my own room. But I absconded on my first day, and when I was caught I was moved to a more restrictive unit, which consisted of two communal rooms and housed roughly twenty boys. Things were always being smashed and there were always riots brewing up in this unit. Bullying was rife. In such a confined space, there was nowhere to go if you wanted to be on your own.

STAFF LIED ABOUT ME TO MY PARENTS
During my six months in care, I was physically and emotionally abused by staff members and pupils. This involved on one occasion being punched in the face for smoking in the dormitory. On another occasion I was thrown into the unit office, pushed to the ground, kicked in the ribs, knelt upon with my left arm yanked

behind my back and sworn at, just for absconding. I also had items stolen from my locker by staff members. If I ever complained, staff members used to humiliate me by calling me names and by encouraging other pupils to bully me. They also used to tell lies about me to my parents and my social worker, claiming that I was a "troublemaker" and a "persistent liar" and that I needed "whipping into shape".

CAMPAIGN FOR AN INQUIRY

These experiences affected me for a long time after I had left care and I didn't know who to trust. I received no support from any quarters. Then, a year after I had left, I read the local newspaper and found that a local councillor was campaigning for an inquiry into allegations of abuse at the school. I contacted the councillor straight away and he agreed to meet me. He listened to my complaints and decided that I should make a statement to the Secretary of State.

I've found there is a stigma attached to being an ex-care child.

The Secretary of State ordered an enquiry to be held by a committee of local councillors. I agreed to give evidence before the committee, but I felt intimidated as it seemed they were having difficulty believing me. It didn't help that I was the only former pupil giving evidence. The councillor was excellent in supporting me and championing my cause. The help he gave me made me realise that there are decent, genuine people around.

The enquiry submitted a report listing numerous recommendations for improving the school. These had to be implemented during a six month period or the Council would withdraw funding for the school. Although none of the staff members who abused me have been brought to justice yet, I did get some things changed for current pupils at my former school by speaking out.

I'VE FOUGHT AND I'VE WON

I left care with no education, as do seventy-five per cent of care leavers. But, with the encouragement of a former teacher, a year later I enrolled at a college of further education. I got five GCSEs and then went on to take four A' levels. I got three grade As and a B.

These past five years haven't been easy. I've found there is a stigma attached to being an ex-care child. Employers, landlords and colleges are often reluctant to give you a chance and you have to work that bit harder to prove yourself.

I am now reading Law at University and acting as an advocate for VCC, enabling thers to get their voices heard.

But I've fought and I've won, and I now have the self-confidence to succeed in whatever I do. Having been written off by Social Services, the police and my own parents as worthless scum, I am now reading Law at University and acting as an advocate for VCC, enabling others to get their voices heard.

Who's Going To Listen?

I made a complaint about last week
And I've heard nothing back not even a squeak

So now I might as well live life on, while the
staff nag nag on.
I'll sit here and think, "Some day I'll be gone".

They have their good days
They have their bad

They say I have attitude
And then they get mad

Then they stop listening
And that makes me sad

So what can I do to be understood?
Try to speak nicely and try to be good?
Or just be myself and say what I mean

And cut out the swearing and keep it all clean
Then maybe they'll listen then things will change

Then my life will get better and things rearrange.

Matthew Aged 15

Getting Help

RECOMMENDATIONS MADE BY SHOUT FOR ACTION

We have discussed numerous issues about being in care in our group – Shout for Action – and with other groups of young people. The issues which concern young people are normally everyday issues. They are not normally about major child abuse and the kinds of things which get headlines. Looked After children are the same as other children but are more vulnerable and need additional support and safeguards. This is born out by our stories. Social workers should visit regularly and away from the placement to ensure a measure of freedom to talk.

This book is about getting heard, the difficulties, and how young people can overcome them. Below we set our recommendations concerning being heard. Nevertheless, there have been some general themes which have come up continually in our discussions which we want to emphasise.

- **Education** is the key that can unlock the door to the future and give self respect.
- **Moving young people** from place to place unnecessarily and against their wishes, sometimes just to reduce spending, must be stopped.
- **Providing emotional support** as well as accommodation and practical help for teenagers, who cannot live at home or who are leaving care, are all crucial.

Having a say about day-to-day issues
Young people need to be able to speak out about day to day concerns as well as the more sensational issues. They need to feel in control of their own lives.

Having a say in decisions about your life
Young people should be involved in all the decisions being taken about their life. When it comes to care planning and review meetings, the professionals should remember whose review it is. The young person should have a say about how meetings are organised and be an active participant. They should be able to read and keep the records and everything should be properly explained.

Young people having adults they can trust

Carers and social workers should all be professionals with clear standards. When in care, young people should be able to choose who would be most helpful to them in any given situation. The adults responsible for the care of young people should be clear about the level of confidentiality they can offer and when they need to pass on information.

The right to have the support of an advocate

If young people want to talk to someone who is outside the situation, they should have the right of access to a professional service which supplies independent advocates. Advocates can support young people, speak up about their concerns and will ensure they know their rights under the Children Act.

Information about rights and how Social Services works

Young people should receive information about their rights all the time they are Looked After and it should be clear and free from jargon. At every review this should be checked. Included in this should be information about how they can get help – helplines, refuges and independent advocacy.

Information about the Complaints Procedure

Young people should be given clear information about their right to complain and be encouraged to do so. They should be made aware that the procedure can be used to challenge decisions when they disagree with them. Young people must be given support with the process.

Complaints should be taken seriously

Every complaint should be recognised as a complaint, answered promptly and considered independently. Young people should be supported by an advocate and offered confidentiality.

Shout for Action believes there has to be a culture shift to respect children's rights and ensure their views are listened to. **Children's Rights should not be a dirty word, they should be above politics – Children's Rights are God-given.**

WHAT ARE YOUR RIGHTS?

INTRODUCTION

This section is about your rights when you are in care. We use the term 'in care' to cover young people who are in care under a care order or those who are in accommodation without having been to court. Most rights are the same but where there are differences we say so.

Most of your rights in care are in the Children Act 1989. This is the law which means that social services have to obey what it says. Usually you can make a complaint or go to court if they do not do so.

Even though your rights might seem quite clear the law can be complicated especially when there are different points of view about what it means. If you are unclear about anything it is very important that you discuss this with someone who can help you.

In the next section we give details about useful organisations who you can contact.

YOUR CARE PLAN

- Social services must make sure that they look after you properly in all **decisions** about your care (section 22(3), Children Act 1989).
- Social services must listen to you and take into account your views about any decisions they make about you (section 22(4)(a)-(5)(a), Children Act 1989). They will give more weight to your views the older you are but they do not have to follow your wishes.
- They must also take into account the views of your parents and any other people who are significant in your life as well as taking into account your race, religion, culture and language (section 22(4)-(5), Children Act 1989).
- Social services must make a written **care plan** when you

come into care. They must consult with you and your parents (see above). You should be given a copy of your care plan written in a way that you understand (paragraph 2.64, Children Act Guidance and Regulations 1991, volume 3). If you are 16 and have asked to be accommodated your care plan should be agreed with you (regulation 3(3), Arrangements for placement of Children (General) Regulations 1991).

YOUR REVIEW

- Social services must hold a **review** about you four weeks after coming into care; the second review must take place within three months and afterwards at six monthly intervals (regulation 3, Review of Children's Cases Regulations 1991). The purpose of the review is to discuss your care plan and to update it. Social services must take into account your wishes and feelings and you should normally be invited to take part in the meeting (regulation 7(1-(2), Review of Children's Cases Regulations 1991).

BEING MOVED

- Social services cannot move you without taking into account your wishes and feelings about this (section 22(4)-(5), Children Act 1989). For more information see 'your care plan' and 'your review'.

YOUR CARE

In a children's home

- You must be allowed to practice your religion including being given the right food and being allowed to wear suitable clothes (regulation 11, Children's Homes Regulations 1991).
- You should be allowed to buy your own clothes (regulation 13, Children's Regulations 1991).
- You should be given enough food which is properly prepared and nutritious (regulation 12, Children's Homes Regulations 1991).
- You are not allowed to be **punished** in the following ways:
  - hit, slapped, pinched, squeezed, shaken, dealt with roughly or have things thrown at you
  - stopped from having food or drink
  - stopped from seeing your parents, family or friends or

from receiving or sending letters or telephone calls

- stopped from getting in touch with your social worker or solicitor
- made to wear clothes that draw attention to yourself
- stopped from having your usual medicines or going to the doctor or dentist when you need to
- given any other form of medication
- deliberately stopped from going to sleep
- made to pay a fine (unless it is a court fine) but up to two thirds of your pocket money could be kept from you
  (regulation 8, Children's Homes Regulations 1991).

In foster care

- You must be visited by a social worker who you should see on your own. The first visit should be one week after your placement and then every six weeks during your first year and afterwards every three months (regulation 6, Foster Placement (Children) Regulations 1991).
- You are not allowed to be **punished** in the following ways:
  - hit, slapped, pinched, squeezed, shaken, dealt with roughly or have things thrown at you (regulation 3(6) and schedule 2, paragraph 5, Foster Placement (Children) Regulations 1991)
  - stopped from having food and drink
  - stopped from having contact with your family and friends
    (paragraph 3.30, Children act Guidance and Regulations, Volume 3).

EDUCATION

- You have the right to education. Social services have responsibility for making sure that you go to school or are being suitably educated at home (section 7, Education Act 1996).

HEALTH

- You have the right to agree to your own medical treatment when you are 16 or if you are younger when the health workers think you have 'sufficient understanding'. This includes contraception (Section 8, Family Law Act 1969; Gillick).
- You normally have a right to say no to medical treatment when you are 16 or if you are younger when the health

workers think you have 'sufficient understanding'. However your parents, the care authority or the courts may over-ride your refusal but this is likely to happen only in life threatening situations or if you are mentally ill.

KEEPING IN TOUCH WITH FAMILY AND FRIENDS

- Social services must try to help you keep in touch with your parents and anyone else significant in your life unless they think that contact is harmful to you or possibly other children (Schedule 2, paragraph 15, Children Act 1989).

- Where you are on a care order social services must allow you reasonable contact with your parents or someone who had a residence order on you before you were in care (section 34(1) Children Act 1989). Social services must not stop your contact without first going to court unless you are in immediate danger (section 34(7), Children Act 1989). You can apply to the court for contact with other people (section 34(2), Children Act 1989).

- Social services may pay for you to visit your family or friends or for them to visit you if you would not be able to visit them otherwise (schedule 2, paragraph 16, Children Act 1989).

- If you are unhappy with arrangements for contact you have a right to go to court.

YOUR RIGHT TO PROTECTION AND SAFETY

- You have a right to be kept safe in care or accommodation. If you have been mistreated in any way you should talk to someone you can trust and get advice from one of the organisations in the next section.

- Social services must look into ways to ensure your safety if they are told or suspect that you have been abused or are at serious risk in any other way or may be in the future. Social services must carry out this duty if you are under 18 and unsafe **wherever** you are living (section 47, Children Act 1989).

RESTRAINT

- Social workers and others looking after you can use reasonable force to prevent immediate danger of physical injury to you or another person or to avoid immediate danger to property.

BEING LOCKED UP

- If you are under 13 you can never be locked up unless the Government gives special permission (regulation 3, Children (Secure Accommodation) Regulations 1991)
- If you are 13 or over you can be locked up only if :
  - you have a history of running away, you are likely to run away again and you are at risk of serious harm or
  - if you are not locked up you are likely to hurt yourself or other people (section 25(1), Children Act).
  - Social services can allow you to be locked up for up to three days but they must go to court if they think you should be locked up for longer (section 10, Children (Secure Accommodation) Regulations).

WANTING TO GO HOME

- If you are accommodated you can go home if your parents agree and social services think this is safe (section 20(8)-(11), Children Act 1989).
- If you are on a care order you can go back to court to ask for the order to be discharged (section 39 Children Act 1989).

NOT WANTING TO GO HOME

- If you are accommodated you can ask your social worker to go to court for a Care Order or Emergency Protection Order but they may not agree to this.
- If you are accommodated and 16 or over you do not have to go home at your parents request. (section 20(8)-(11), Children Act 1989).

LEAVING CARE

- Your rights in care last until you are 18 (section 105, Children Act 1989).
- Before you leave care, social services must help you get ready for the time when you leave, whether you go home or go on to live independently (section 24((1), Children Act 1989).
- All social services departments must have information about their leaving care policies (paragraph 2(a) schedule 2, Children Act 1989).
- The Government has said that it wants to make sure that

young people leaving care are not isolated and can join in socially and economically as citizens (Objectives for Social Services for Children, Department of Health, 1998).

- If you leave care after you are 16, social services must give you **advice** until you are 21 if they think that you are in need and you have asked for help (sections 24(2) – (5) Children Act 1989).

- Social services may also give you **assistance** (section 24(6) Children Act 1989) **in the following ways:**

Money They may give you cash but the law says only 'in exceptional circumstances'. Local authorities are encouraged to give leaving care grants. They should also look at your individual welfare needs in deciding whether to give you money in other circumstances (paragraphs 9.70 -9.71, Children Act Guidance and Regulations, Volume 3).

Housing At 16 and 17, social services must provide you with accommodation if you are homeless or at risk of being made homeless and if they believe that you are in serious danger (section 20(3) Children Act 1989)

Education and training Social services may help towards your living expenses if you continue your education or training and they may also give you a grant. They may also help with your living expenses if you are working or looking for work (section 24(8)-(9), Children Act 1989).

SEEING YOUR FILES

- If social services think that you have 'sufficient understanding' you have a right to see what is written about you on your social work file. You will not be able to see things written about other people unless they give permission for this and there are certain other exemptions (regulation 8, Access to Personal Files Regulations 1989 and paragraph 40, Local Authority Circular, LAC(89)(2)).

MAKING A COMPLAINT

- You have a right to make a complaint if you disagree with the plans for you or you are unhappy about anything (section 26, Children Act 1989).
- There are three stages to the complaints procedure:

Stage 1: People who work with you should try to resolve your complaint

Stage 2: formal investigation carried out by a senior officer of social services who is not involved with you or your family along with an independent person who does not work for social services and whose job is to make sure that everything is being done fairly. They should each write a report and social services should give you their recommendations within four weeks of the start of stage two (regulation 6, Representations Procedure (Children) Regulations 1991).

Stage 3: if you are unhappy with these recommendations you have the right to ask for a complaints review panel to consider your complaints. It must meet within four weeks and you have the right to attend (regulation 8, Representations Procedure (Children) Regulations 1991). The panel must make its decision within 24 hours (regulation 9, Representations Procedure (Children) Regulations 1991).

- If you are still dissatisfied you can make a further complaint to the Local Government Ombudsman.

USEFUL CONTACTS

HELPLINES
ChildLine
All children: Freephone **0800 11 11**
Children in care: Freephone **0800 88 44 44**
**5.30 – 9.30 pm Monday – Friday
4.00 – 8.00 pm Saturday and Sunday**

Who Cares? Trust
Linkline: Freephone 0500 564 570
or write to: The Who Cares? Trust, Kemp House, 152-160 City Road, London EC1V 2NP.
Also publish Who Cares? Magazine, produced for and by young people in public care.

NSPCC
Child Protection Helpline: Freephone 0800 800 500 the phone is answered by Child Protection telephone counsellors who talk to social services and other statutory agencies if you give information about abuse and your name and address.

ADVOCACY
Voice for the Child in Care (VCC)   0171 833 5792
Covers the London area (and has some local schemes across England). You can telephone ChildLine when the office is closed.

National Youth Advocacy Service (NYAS) 0151 342 7852
Covers England and Wales
Freephone (by arrangement with ChildLine) **0800 61 61 01**
**3.30 – 9.30 pm Monday to Friday
2.00 – 8.00 pm Saturday and Sunday**

Wales Advocacy Unit – The Children's Society
Freephone   **0800 581 862**
Telephone advice and advocacy service for Wales

Prison Boy

Prison boy, my knees were shaking
Prison boy, my heart was breaking
The judge was harsh, didn't say a lot
But five long years was what you got.

Prison boy, why did you nick
From an old, weak man, it made me sick
You took his wallet, all his money
It made me cry, you thought it was funny.

Prison boy, you tied him up
Wrecked his home, and kicked his pup
You thought you were such a macho man
But when he fought back, you turned and ran.

Prison boy, you next tried drugs
Didn't hear when I said "that's just for mugs"
From crime to crime you left your mark
Under cover of the dark.

Prison boy, you stabbed a mate
Who dared to be a little late
On the night you planned to rob a bank
When I heard what you'd done my heart sank.

You went and did it anyway
You thought my heart would be here to stay
I'm sorry love, you did it wrong
Now you have to sing your prison song.

Gemma Aged 15